CLIMBING PLANTS AND WALL SHRUBS

Stephen Taffler

CROWOOD GARDENING GUIDES

First published in 1990 by
The Crowood Press
Gipsy Lane, Swindon,
Wiltshire SN2 6DQ

British Library Cataloguing in Publication Data

Taffler, Stephen
    Climbing plants.
    I. Gardens. Climbing plants & shrubs
    I. Title
    635.97

    ISBN 1 85223 165 3

Acknowledgements
My thanks are due to many people and I readily acknowledge my use of the
writings of others which have been of great assistance. In particular, those books
which have helped me with the finer points of nomenclature.
I wish to record my gratitude to my wife, Gill, for her help and advice on
various aspects of this book, particularly for preparing the manuscript.

Photographs by Stephen Taffler
Line illustrations by Claire Upsdale-Jones.

Typeset by Avonset, Midsomer Norton, Bath.
Printed and bound by Times Publishing Group, Singapore.

Contents

Preface

It is my pleasure to dedicate this book to you, the reader. I hope that you will be sufficiently enthused to go out and buy climbing plants and shrubs that will add a new, vertical dimension to your garden.

Fig 1   A winding path through an herbaceous border. The ground is clothed right through to the background of trees, thus suppressing weeds and providing year round colour and texture.

This book is intended to be 'user friendly', for the beginner who is seeking to cover boundary walls and house walls, pergolas and arbours, or to use plants to provide screening for buildings and sheds.

To acquire plants is a simple matter, the challenge is to grow them successfully. Study their requirements and endeavour to provide the favourable conditions that will enable them to repay you with their foliage and flower. A spade and fork, a good pair of secateurs, good loam and peat, some slow-acting fertiliser such as bone meal, are all that is needed to produce rewarding results.

To avoid any misunderstanding, it is necessary to state at the outset that the purpose of this book is to deal only with those climbing plants and wall shrubs suited to those with a limited experience of gardening but who wish to broaden their horizons. No claim is made that all the climbing and trailing plants known to cultivation are included. Those mentioned are a selection and, in the opinion of the author, are desirable either for their flower, leaf shape or seasonal colour and for the fact that some are evergreen and, in the main, hardy or tolerably so in most parts of the country. Their cultivation is relatively easy if the simple guide-lines laid down in this book are followed. Where a plant is not totally hardy, even when grown in the protection of a wall or fence, mention of this is made in the descriptive notes.

Patience is a vital ingredient. Many climbing plants take several seasons to really start covering a wall or pergola, but it is worth the wait. One cannot hurry nature to produce the desired effect.

CHAPTER 1

Introduction

Climbing roses round the door with honeysuckle and perhaps clematis framing windows seem to be part of the ideal garden that so many of us wish to achieve.

Doorways and gates into the garden should be made as attractive and inviting as possible. Think of staging an effect, preparing the eyes of one's friends for the delights of the garden that you have created and giving great pleasure to those who share this plot with you. So often, these entrances are thought of (if at all) as the only practical way to go to and from the garden. Try to give them some importance and let them play a role in the overall picture. Walls or gates can be given an archway of trellis at the top, or welded iron could be used and clothed with climbing plants that have striking foliage or flowers. This sets the scene and everyone should realise what a treat is in store for them visually and if you have chosen, for instance, honeysuckle, jasmine or wisteria, there is the added bonus of the scented air.

There are great possibilities in planting even the smallest of gardens. By planting the outer edges of the garden and by using various types of structure such as trellis, fences etc for climbing and trailing plants more planting area than was possibly first thought will be available. The roots and stems of clematis, roses, honeysuckle and other like plants take up comparatively little room, and all the growth, foliage and flowers are on the stems and at the top of whatever structure you have built. This leaves room for underplanting with bulbs and ornamental shrubs.

Look at your garden with fresh eyes. Look at the house walls, the fences and the outbuildings. Here is a marvellous opportunity to use these vertical planes to add dimension, interest and colour. When flowering is over some climbing plants have the compensation of leaves giving superb autumn colour, and thus extending the season. In the case of ivies, these are mainly evergreen and to my mind, there is nothing more charming than to see birds nesting and rearing their young in the more mature plantings, in

Fig 2   A good example of planting against the wall of an outbuilding.

springtime. When ivies have reached the top of their climbing support, they become arborescent (adult). They will then flower and fruit and late-season bees and birds love this harvest.

To many people, the garden is a haven of peace from which we try to banish the outside world. Here we can plan hidden corners where the plants that we particularly treasure can be grown, whether it be for their leaf form, colour or flower. A sense of mystery within a garden is a delight – one should never be able to see a garden all at once. By using arches, pergolas and winding paths, fragrant and cascading plants will induce a mood of calm, a place where one can feel that all is well with the world. A place to give one time to think of little else except perhaps to

Fig 3   The summer house or gazebo can often be simply constructed at home and provides excellent areas for climbing plants.

notice where a wandering stem on one of the climbing plants needs a little coaxing back into place, or one or two of the roses need a little gentle de-heading – nothing strenuous – just putting your garden world to rights.

While you are noticing these little things, you must have somewhere to sit and drink in the sights and sounds of the garden. The seat can be as simple as a smooth piece of wood or a plank supported by bricks, perhaps of the ornamental type used for garden walls. In garden centres, there are many garden seats to be seen – some in teak, others in reproduction eighteenth century or Victorian styles that have curved ironwork as supports. There are also stone benches which, to the eye, have an attractive look but these can feel very hard and take time to dry out after rain.

Ideally, the paths in the garden should not be of regular shaped and sized paving slabs. They bear too much resemblance to the streets that we have to use every day. Plan the paths so that they wind, try not to have straight lines, and try to make them an interesting feature.

Old and mellow brick or stone walls give a lovely sense of security and calm. Their very colours are pleasing and because they retain warmth from the sun, shelter is provided for plants to flourish. Often plants from the warmer Mediterranean countries can be grown and enjoyed in the colder climate of Britain. When grown against a south wall, there is an opportunity for growing some unusual and special plants. Walls can also be used to encompass many other plants which, although not really climbers, are plants that benefit from being trained against a

Fig 4   A peaceful corner, the white wall clothed with climbers.

wall and tied in, and which otherwise would make a bush or small tree if grown in open space.

Of course, very few people have the good fortune to have a garden with the benefit of such walls. Most will have to create that same feeling in an open plot with little shape or scope in aspect. To change the character of such a plot can be a challenge but it can be a most enjoyable task if carefully planned. To erect walls or fences can be fairly expensive but it may be worth sacrificing some luxury in order to do this.

There are less expensive ways of achieving the effect that you wish. Very attractive boundary fences can be made using readily available 1.8m (6ft) long panels of close-boarded wooden fencing. Today, manufacturers can offer at least ten different designs including vertical-boarded, close-lapped, horizontal-boarded and so on. Such close-boarded fences not only act as windbreaks but also screen you from your neighbours. These panels can be obtained in varying heights from 1.2m (4ft) upwards and can incorporate 0.3m (1ft) or 0.6m (2ft) panels of trellis at the top. There are recently introduced modern designs which have a curved top rail to the trellis, with the curve reaching from a 1.2m (4ft) point up the panel on to a 1.8m (6ft) point at the posts. Conversely, they can be obtained with a curve in the centre of the panel going down to the posts. These trellises can thus be arranged with many attractive designs in mind. Very simple and practical fences can be made using whole or split bamboo canes. In certain areas of the country, you can readily find wattle hurdles of hazel or willow that make a pleasant background and also have the advantage of spacing between the weaving which facilitate the tying in and training of plants.

Some of you will have established chain-link boundary fencing. Do not despair. While this type of fencing can look unappealing for the first few years, climbing plants can be chosen for a particular attribute e.g. their satisfying speed of growth, and used imaginatively, such plants conceal their support and make, in effect, a 'fedge', a coined word meaning a cross between a fence and a hedge.

Fig 5   An example of a trellis using bamboo.

Climbing and wall plants are the keynote plants that tune the perception of a visitor's true appreciation of the spirit of the garden. They can completely transform the garden atmosphere and in hot weather, they give a feeling of coolness as well as practical shade from the sun.

To paraphrase an old maxim, the garden should run up and embrace the house, thus making the house and garden one home.

I promise you that climbing plants will reward you and give much pleasure, softening the hard outlines of man-made structures and they will help to create a world of your own – an oasis within your own garden.

CHAPTER 2

What is a Climber?

In the wild, climbers use adjacent shrubs and trees to reach for light and air. The growths work their way up through the host plant's branches, hooking, coiling and turning their way, often with 'hold fasts' or with tenacious rootlets like ivies. We can emulate the natural growth habit by training our climbers up wires, fences, trellis and arbours and by 'tying in' as they grow.

We can therefore say that a climber is taken to mean a plant that needs some form of support if it is not to lie on the ground. Some are scramblers rather than true climbers and some are more properly described as trailing plants. If you have the space, many climbers can be planted deliberately without support and many behave like trailing plants and provide effective ground cover. Examples of this method of growing may be seen at Hilliers Arboretum, in Ampfield, Winchester, where small flowered species clematis very effectively scramble along the ground or over small shrubs.

The recommended list also includes wall shrubs as most walls provide shelter and some extra warmth for plants and thus enable them to flourish in a colder climate than that from which they originate. Often, plants originating from the Mediterranean area can be grown and enjoyed in many parts of Great Britain. A south wall provides an opportunity for growing some unusual and special plants. Walls can also be used to encompass many other plants which, although they are not really climbers, do benefit from being trained against a wall and tied in. These plants would otherwise make a bush or small tree if grown in the open.

Rhamnus alaternus 'Variegata' is one such example. This is almost totally evergreen and its

Fig 6 Rosmarinus officinalis *'Aureus'. The gilded Rosemary. This has been known to collectors of unusual plants for many years, possibly back to Tudor times.*

9

Fig 7   An ideal honeysuckle with large terminal clusters of flowers, an eye-catcher for a shady site.

variegated leaves are pleasantly edged with white. The normal all green leaved *Rhamnus* is quite hardy when grown from the Wash downwards, but the variegated plant needs the protection of a wall if it is to be grown in the open, even in the south, where the young, tender growths and leaves might be damaged in the frosts of a hard winter. There are many forms of *Hedera helix* – ivy – with yellow or white variegations on the leaves. These are particularly valuable and attractive in the dull days of winter as they are evergreen. A varied selection of ornamental plants will also bring interest at different times of the year.

CHAPTER 3

Observations on Gardening History

'How deeply seated in the human heart is the liking for gardens and gardening.'

Alexander Smith
1830–1867

The 'mother' of modern-day gardening as a hobby and leisure activity was undoubtedly Gertrude Jekyll. It was she who showed us how to break away from the stereotyped and accepted ways of garden planning. This was in contrast to the great gardens of the wealthy, bringing gardens and gardening down to a more common level.

The well-known gardening writer, Graham Stuart Thomas OBE, decided at the early age of eight years old, to make gardening his career and like many others, I consider him to be *the* authority on all aspects of gardening. His many books are most enjoyable to read and in one of these, *The Art of Gardening*, he tells us that it was during Elizabethan days that gardening was confined to small courtyards, walled areas and other enclosures.

In the latter half of the last century, new plants streamed into England from Europe, the Middle East, Africa, the whole of the American Continent and from the Far East. Many of these plants make excellent subjects for clothing walls and other structures allowing the plants the benefit of shelter, and thus enhancing the colour and form of their flowers for us to enjoy.

There have been several distinct styles of gardening over the last three hundred years. Garden design owes much to ancient symbolism which becomes more pronounced as one moves East – Chinese and Japanese gardens are very formal. For definition we must go back to the beginning of agriculture. Man began to cultivate plants when he lived in settled communities and had progressed from his need to subsist on hunting and collecting wild vegetable material. Earliest cultivators seem to have lived about 8000 BC and farming can be traced back to around 6500 BC. Organised cultivation was practised in South America about 2500 BC generally around villages.

At some point in village evolution, houses came to have walled or fenced enclosures, probably initially to pen in goats and sheep. The seedling fig or vine provided welcome shade for the animals and probably for the house owner.

A Sumarian legend speaks of a diligent gardener who, when setting out his plant beds, found that high winds blew sand from the mountains and destroyed his garden. When the gods were consulted, he was told to plant his garden with trees to provide both shelter and shade. The original windbreak?

The garden, closely associated with a house, is almost always an indication of an advanced civilisation. This, together with the rule of law becoming more effective, meant that the danger of local wars and marauding bands lessened. Fortifications which had consisted of high walls and wide moats could thus be reduced, allowing the owners of houses to spread their gardens and their buildings to look out on to the surrounding countryside, rather than looking inwards to their own courtyards. At this time, the use of

11

Fig 8   Plants tucked into step edges, thus clothing the steps and the risers.

decorative plants increased as opposed to those for purely utilitarian use.

Taking advantage of the hitherto undeveloped countryside, the houses of those who were better off began to have individual gardens. Many towns and villages were also built after the need for fortification had dwindled. Throughout history, most gardens have been divided into different parts, each with distinct functions. Quite apart from the utility areas, there were sections for various diversions, for privacy and for the basic pleasure of scene changes, to surprise and delight visitors.

To trace the development of gardens in different cultures and ages, one must bear in mind the main purpose for which gardens have been designed, that is, pleasure – from the simplest levels of enjoying shade and coolness to those of appreciating plants and flowers for their beauty.

In modern times, early Dutch settlers in America were perhaps the most efficient agriculturists and gardeners. They took with them many ornamental plants and began to cultivate the finer species of the wild plants that they found there.

Once it was understood that plants must be a certain distance apart to give adequate light, they became separated by trodden areas – paths – which brought formality, straight lines, squares and rectangles. Part of this formality derived from the need to irrigate with the maximum economy of water and channelling, hence simple rectangular forms. The raising of such beds was not simply ornamental but was to assist drainage.

The craft of gardening has always involved a great deal of work and much of this has been devoted to the essential need for growing food. Once the gardener has some leisure, he can then

12

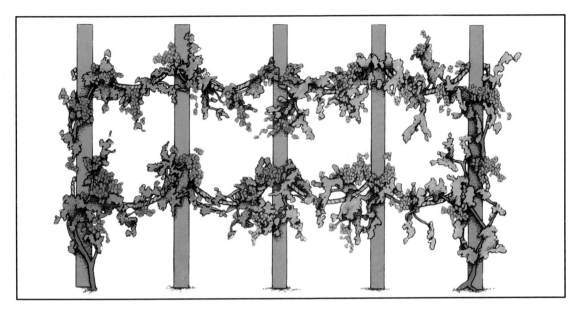

Fig 9   Climbers can be trained up pillars or along swags of rope by pruning to encourage lateral growths.

cultivate plants for diversion and decoration. By doing so, he joins in nature's creative process, making his own life more satisfying. Many garden owners today are their own designers and are probably less influenced by fashion than were the wealthier creators of grand gardens in earlier times. The ardent plantsmen of today are those who garden with their own labour and only use the minimum of help. The particular needs of each plant is studied to ensure that it is given the best possible conditions.

Graham Stuart Thomas is of the opinion that those who plant gardens can primarily be divided into three fairly clear-cut categories. There is the collector, the artist plantsman and the landscape architect. The collector and the artist plantsman are probably more evident in Britain than elsewhere and this is perhaps because our climate enables us to grow an almost unparalleled range of plants from all over the world. However, as that famous gardener, Gertrude Jekyll, wrote in 1908 in her book *Colour Schemes for the Flower Garden*, 'the possession of a quantity of plants, however good the plants may be themselves and however ample their number, does not make a garden; it only makes a collection.' She also went on to say that 'having got the plants, the great thing is to use them with careful selection and definite intention'.

This, of course, is very easy to say but not always easy to apply. What you should do is to get to know your plants, find out the conditions they prefer, how to grow them and where to grow them. The next step is to decide how to arrange them so as to give you the utmost pleasure with their foliage, flower and scent and combining this with the plant's own needs for ideal conditions. Take time to study these requirements as plant associations are important. After all, it is pointless to place a low growing plant at the back of one that has a taller growth habit. Likewise, think of the colours; do they blend or do they shout at one another? In some gardens, one can see some horrendous colour associations – hot pinks, blazing orange, magenta, mauve, all massed together without much thought and creating a dazzling but unpleasing effect.

13

CHAPTER 4

Cultivated Plants for Pleasure

In common with all plants, climbers and trailers need good soil in which to grow. One of the chief causes of poor results is the lack of preparation at the start.

Unlike other plants grown elsewhere in the garden, most climbers are more or less permanent occupants of the chosen site. Once planted, it is best not to disturb them at their base but allow them to root and grow as freely as possible. Once they have got a satisfactory start, the roots will spread under gravelled or even flagged walks quite happily. Clematis particularly like a cool root run and in fact I recommend placing a slab, or a slate or two, around their roots to keep these cool and moist.

Many climbers, particularly roses and clematis, can produce a great deal of flower often over a long season. Here again, I impress upon you, that the more careful the preparation of the soil, the better the results will be.

SOIL

A little knowledge and understanding of the soil in your garden can be very helpful. Is it acid, neutral or alkaline? A small soil-testing kit can be purchased from your garden centre and, following the instructions, it will tell you the pH value. Accept the findings and realise that you will not be able to grow some plants unless you are fortunate enough to find that your soil is neutral.

Thus, if you want to grow acid-loving plants, you can always enrich the soil with peats that test to acid. It is more difficult should your soil be strongly alkaline, that is, chalky, to be successful with such plants. One can practise the alternative of gardening with raised beds of peat soil placed over black polythene sheets to prevent the ingress of lime, through capillary action, from the lower soil. This is a specialist way of growing to surmount difficulties and enabling particular plants to be grown. However, the subject is really deserving of separate reading and your local library will have books dealing with gardening on chalky soils.

If you do garden on chalky soil, accept the situation and enjoy the plants that will grow well. Clematis do very well in this soil as do ivies and certain roses and there are other plants mentioned in the plant list in this book.

It can therefore be appreciated what an important part soil plays in the successful culture of plants. There are other soils that you may encounter. Sandy soils provide excellent drainage but are thin in nourishment and you will need to enrich with ample supplies of rotted compost, moisture-retaining peat and, if your pocket will allow, liberal use of spent hops. There is also spent mushroom compost which can be obtained by the sack or load quite cheaply if your garden is near a mushroom farm. This is usually a mixture of horse manure, rotted straw and peat but do remember that mushroom farmers add a liberal amount of chalk to their mushroom beds in order to grow their crops successfully. Therefore, the end product will contain a certain amount of lime.

Fig 10   A good mulch suppresses weeds, feeds the plant and conserves
moisture in the soil.

In nearly all gardening, plants resent water-logged soil. For those gardening on clay, the biggest problems are probably drainage and waterlogging. Here I recommend the digging in, to a prepared planting site, of quantities of horticultural sharp grit to provide drainage. This should be free of clay sand particles. Beware of builders sand which invariably has a content of fine particle clays which will only add to the problem as it will be washed down through the soil. Providing that the clay soil is not waterlogged, roses will do you well in this material. Clay tends to dry out and crack in excessively dry periods, so dig in damp peat, moisture retaining composts and other humus. It is advisable to mulch heavily with humus-rich material. Lastly, once improved, the soil must not be abandoned, but topped up from year to year by adding mulches of humus-rich material. Very popular now as a mulch or top dressing are various grades and sizes of bark chippings. These have the advantage also of looking most attractive and will suppress the growth of annual weeds.

Peat has the effect of liberating acids that precipitate the clay colloids and reduces the obstinate, sticky qualities of the soil by holding the clay particles apart, giving the young roots of plants an easy start. Use it as liberally as possible.

Peat is usually purchased sealed in a polythene bag, sack or bale. It is moist to the touch and quite spongy when pressed by the hand. However, a peat bale that has been opened and left to dry out in the elements can often be very difficult to re-dampen. It is good garden husbandry to keep the peat moist at all times. It is also wise to remember that peat has very little

15

food value and needs to be accompanied by a fertiliser, such as bone meal or hoof and horn.

If the preparatory work to the soil can be carried out a month or so before planting, this is an advantage. The soil will then naturally settle and allow bacteria and other organisms to do their work of breaking down the compost and fertilisers that you have placed in the soil.

ASPECT AND SITE

Fortunately, there is a wide selection of plants available that are suitable for all aspects of walls and fences. Whilst there are some plants that definitely prefer a shady position, the majority will thrive equally well on an eastern, western or southern site.

The best of all aspects is undoubtedly south or south-western, particularly for the more tender plants. It provides the beneficial influence of sunshine, which is so essential for the production of well ripened wood as well as a good show of flower. The western wall has the advantage of retaining the accumulated heat of the day, for very often, afternoons are sunnier than mornings.

When you refer to the list of descriptions of climbing and trailing plants, mention is made if a plant needs a particular position or aspect. When no mention is made, it can be assumed that the plant will do equally well on an eastern, western or southern aspect.

It is considered advisable to plant early spring-flowering plants where they will not be subject to early morning sun which has been preceded by a frost. Often flowers are uninjured by a few degrees of frost provided that they can thaw out gradually. When a late frost is followed, as it frequently is, by bright early sunshine, the rapid thawing of the flowers will cause them to be spoilt. It is always worth taking the risk of damage by frost so that you can enjoy the loveliness of early flowering plants. Should you lose the flowers in one spring, there is always next year to look forward to.

Therefore, do not put such tender early plants on an eastern wall or fence. If your choice is limited and you only have this particular aspect available for planting, do not be deterred, but carefully choose later flowering plants for this position.

There are a number of climbers to grow against a north or north-west facing wall or fence

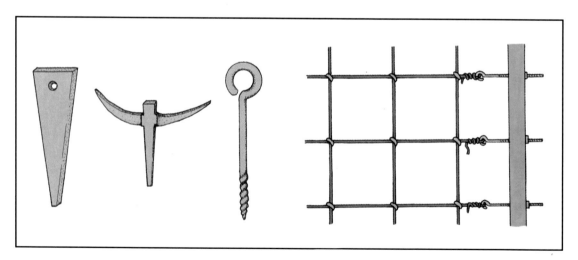

Fig II Climbers need support to cover a wall or fence. The use of wall nails or vine eyes is recommended.

that will thrive without the sun and its warmth. Indeed, there are some that prefer a north aspect. Many trailing plants prefer shade and are at home beneath other larger growing plants. Some are ideal for dense shade, such as beneath trees and naturally, there are those that prefer hot, sunny banks or a low wall.

The usual rule of thumb guide for planting distances between climbers is that they should not be closer than half the ultimate height of the species chosen. This, if taken literally, can be very restricting in a small garden for it limits the number of climbers that you can happily encompass.

I have, for many years, enjoyed planting several climbers that attain 3m (IIft) or more growth in a year such as Clematis, within Im (3.3ft) of each other, and allowed them to intermingle their growths. So too, is it possible to plant an ivy within Im (3.3ft) or even less of a Clematis, but training the ivy over a shrub further out into the border. This may necessitate giving the ivy an annual hair cut when it becomes too rampant, to keep it within bounds. *Tropaeolum tuberosum* 'Ken Aslet' form, will grow happily in poor soil and flower more profusely if its tuber is close by an evergreen wall shrub which will act as its host. There are many combinations of plantings that you can experiment with.

Root systems of climbers adapt and will co-exist with the roots of trees and shrubs but better initial growth will be made if the competition factor can be reduced for the climber. Depending on the tree, the climber could be planted at the base of the tree trunk where the tree's feeding roots are probably non-existent, or it could be planted a metre or so away from the tree's canopy of branches where the feeding roots thin out.

If there is any doubt about the vigour of tree roots, the side of the hole to take the climber can be lined with plastic sheeting but do not line the bottom of the hole. The hole should then be filled with heavily humus-enriched soil which is so essential to give the climber a good start in life.

Fig 12   An example of a home-constructed bamboo trellis for climbing plants.

PREPARING FOR PLANTING

Against the walls of houses or other buildings where the soil is likely to be very poor, a test dig will probably show that the area is full of builders rubble. Further, because the overhang of the roof over the soil (under the eaves), and the house foundations (footings) are likely to be stepped out into the planting area from the main wall structure, the soil, through lack of adequate rain, will probably be dry, under-nourished and lacking in humus.

Bear in mind that it is not wise to plant too near the exposed corner of a building nor indeed too near a drain, as roots can break and block drains. Sites near corners are often rather exposed and evergreen plants very often suffer badly and young foliage may be scorched by persistent winds. Plant a metre or so back from a corner if possible, allowing the plant plenty of room for growth. For boundary walls that have a border in front, it is to be hoped that no new soil or preparation will be needed providing that it has previously been well cultivated.

Whatever the natural soil of your garden, climbing plants growing against a wall need a generous supply of enriched soil. It is most important, if you have the space to work in, to dig out a hole 60×60cm (24×24in). Lay the soil that is dug out on a sheet of polythene or sacking or other clear area. Break up the soil and work in a mixture of peat or other humus-rich material such as composted kitchen waste, leaves, grass etc, or well rotted farmyard manure. Mix in too, a handful of slow acting fertiliser such as bone meal or hoof and horn. Return the soil that was removed and which now will be in far better condition to receive your plant. The soil should be levelled and firmed by light and careful treading before planting. It is most important, and I stress, that as your plant is intended to give you many years of successful foliage and flower, that this soil preparation is thoroughly carried out.

PLANTING

The actual planting is perhaps the easiest and most pleasant of all garden tasks. You have done the hard work of soil preparation and have had the pleasure of choosing and selecting your plant and will have already decided where it should be sited to be seen and enjoyed to its best advantage.

Once a site has been suitably prepared, treat a climbing plant like any other. If your plant has been purchased from a nursery or garden centre, read the label for this might give you quite a lot of information such as the height that the plant will reach, flowering time, what time of year to plant, position for planting and whether it is evergreen. Don't be afraid of asking for advice at the nursery or garden centre but beware of an untrained assistant who may be inexperienced and not knowledgeable about the plants that they are selling. Sometimes it is worth asking the person beside you who is also looking for plants. A great many people are very helpful and can give the benefit of their own experience.

Container or pot grown climbers can be planted at any time of the year, though the favourite times in my experience are autumn and spring. Should you acquire a container grown plant in leaf and flower at any other time of the year, it is still better to plant this in the ground rather than water it in the pot above ground. Left above ground the elements could cause it to dry out rapidly, resulting in the plant suffering neglect and possible demise whilst you are waiting for the preferred planting time.

If you are under pressure with other interests and activities taking your time and preventing proper planting, it is better to heel in the plant, in its pot, into the ground and cover it with a few inches of soil. If the plant is tender in your area, it is wise to plant in the spring rather than nurse it through the first winter when it is barely established.

Once the area for planting has been prepared, make a hole wide enough and deep enough to take the potful of roots. Bear in mind that it is a usual and good practice to plant your climber 30–45cm (11–17in) away from the wall. From this point, the plant can be trained back to the wall via a length of stake or cane and ultimately trained to wires or trellis. Do also bear in mind that this planting position will receive little moisture when it is raining.

If your plant is in a container (a pot or black polythene bag), remove the plant from the pot or cut the bag away and gently tease out the lower roots from the growing point. Position the plant in the hole which should be sufficiently large to receive the root ball so that when properly firmed in, the soil mark on the plant collar will be only slightly below the soil surface. Firm the soil around the roots.

If your plant has remained in the pot too long and the roots have become very congested, these must be gently teased out and spread away from the root ball. Plants that have become very pot bound and have had their roots restricted, rarely grow away so freely as those that have had a less cramped root system. Make sure when buying plants to choose those with healthy, deep green leaves rather than those showing signs of starvation and stress usually due to inadequate watering and maintenance. The yellow chloritic leaves on the plant will warn you of this condition. It is most important to be sure that the soil in the pot is thoroughly moist. If necessary, soak the plant, in its container, in a bucket of water overnight before planting.

AFTER PLANTING

Because the young growths of the plant may be delicate and brittle, encircle the plant with a piece of chicken wire about 30cm (IIin) high and push the wire into the ground to a depth of 2–3cm (Iin). This is further protection for the plant from pets such as cats and dogs.

It is particularly important to realise that when planting in spring the ground often suffers from dry spells, and climbing plants should not be allowed to become dry at the roots. There are no hard and fast rules for watering. Certainly 'water in' your newly planted climber – this has the advantage of settling in the soil around the root ball. Soils, however good, do tend to dry out during the summer and hotter weather and the need to water should be anticipated. Do not assume, that because the rest of the soil in the garden is moist, that the areas beneath walls and fences are in a like condition. Climbing plants

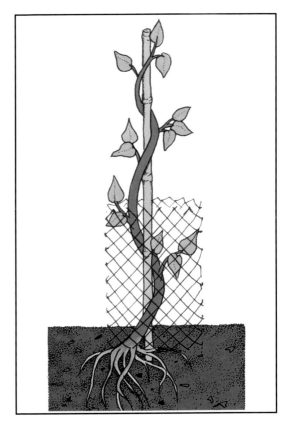

Fig 13 *Young plants may need protection from pets or wildlife. A cylinder of wire netting let into the soil around the plant will act as a guard.*

need plenty of water during the growing season.

Perhaps it is wise to bear in mind that a good drink once a week from heaven or the watering can is a good maxim to follow. Plants that have just been put into the soil are very vulnerable, they appreciate tender, loving care and will reward you for this attention in the years to come.

WINTER PROTECTION

During severe winters, frost and wind can cause a lot of trouble and damage to newly planted specimens. It will be necessary to provide a thick mulch around the base of the plant and some

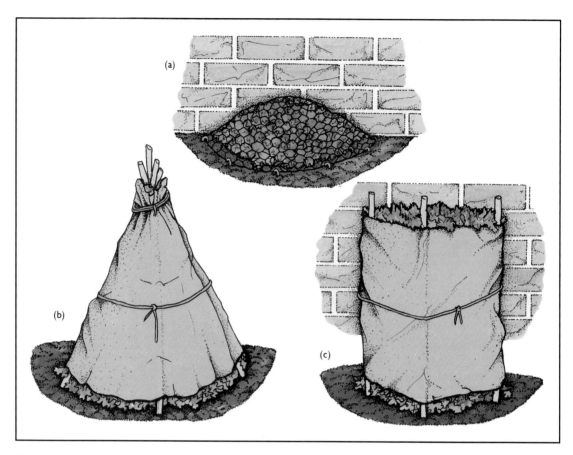

Fig 14   Ways of protecting plants during winter: (a) Protecting the roots with leaves, straw and other litter, covering overall with mesh pegged into the ground; (b) A wigwam of canes wrapped around with polythene sheeting or jute sacking, with the plant safely protected with a blanket of straw, dried leaves etc. Remember to leave space for ventilation at the top and the bottom to allow the circulation of air; (c) An erection of canes and wire mesh or netting to insulate well-trained shrubs with a blanket of leaves, bracken or straw within. Note that the top and bottom are left uncovered to allow for air circulation.

protection up to 1m (3.3ft) of the main stem. It is hoped that new growth will develop in the spring from the protected parts even if the unprotected parts are damaged.

The mulch should be placed around the plant in the autumn which will help to conserve the warmth in the soil and act as an insulation from the forthcoming cold. The mulch should consist of dried leaves, the dried and dead stems of herbaceous plants with added straw or bracken. To

protect the main stem of the plant, make a wigwam of stout twigs and around this, pack a similar mixture of straw, bracken etc. Not everyone can obtain these materials and as an alternative, use a wrapping of hessian, sacking or clear, heavy duty polythene. The double walled 'bubble' polythene is very effective and is obtainable from most garden centres. Do remember however, not to entirely prevent a free circulation of air around the plant as this could cause condensation, allowing fungus and rot to take hold.

Bracken and straw sandwiched between two layers of chicken wire and laced together with galvanised wire can be made into mats and placed around the stem base and pushed up tight to the wall or fence. If you have any fibreglass insulation material, this can be incorporated or used as a substitute, but do wear rubber gloves when handling it.

It should also be remembered that winds, due to the wind chill factor, are often considerably colder than the mean air temperature. Evergreen plants are under particular threat because they continue giving off moisture from their leaves during the winter. Water loss is increased by the wind and if the roots of the plant are frozen, the plant cannot replace the water. This results in 'burning' of the leaves and can even kill the whole plant.

I have known some people use heavy panes of glass, leant against the wall, with bracken or straw packed in at the sides of the glass. The glass had some fixing device at the top to prevent a sudden gust of wind catching it and moving it away from the wall, and probably breaking the glass.

By such means, half hardy plants can be brought through an average hard winter. This particularly applies to young 'suspect' hardy climbers. The same plants will, when older, in all probability withstand all but a very severe frost reasonably well.

CONTAINERS, POTS AND TUBS

Climbers can be grown in containers placed against walls, but they will need adequate water and nourishment. The plants will need support, either from within the container or from the wall behind their position.

Where it is not practical to plant at the foot of such walls due, for instance, to paths adjacent to the brickwork, one can add colour by planting

Fig 15   Colourful geraniums grown in a pot.

window boxes, wall pots and hanging baskets to the walls of the house, balcony or garage. Using containers, a very pleasing effect is to be had by allowing plants to hang down and trail. Here, the hanging basket comes into its own by forming a collection hung from the spars of a pergola or car-port. This makes an excellent, unusual and colourful feature.

CHAPTER 5

The Supporting Role

Support may be gained from walls, fences, tripods, poles, trellis, arbours, pergolas, archways, or whatever else is to hand – maybe an existing old shed or a neighbour's outbuilding. These can all be covered by a living, growing curtain. You are the designer and can make of it whatever you will.

Whatever the support chosen for the climber, remember that climbing plants with stems, leaves, flowers and in some cases, older wood,

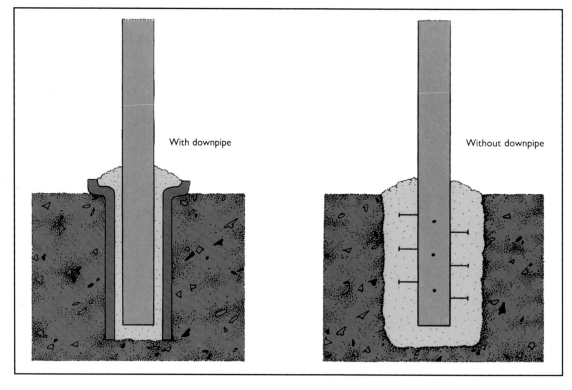

Fig 16 The more conventional method of erecting fence and trellis posts by digging out holes and inserting creosote-treated posts. Use the strongest fencing posts that you can afford. This will save much time and trouble in possible gale force conditions.

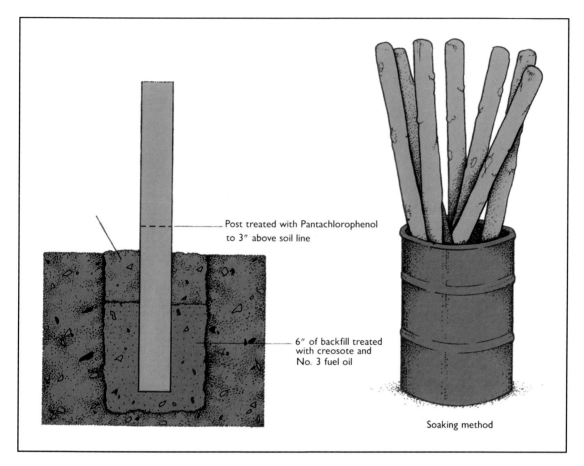

Post treated with Pantachlorophenol to 3″ above soil line

6″ of backfill treated with creosote and No. 3 fuel oil

Soaking method

Fig 17   Preserving the underground portion of wooden posts.

can be exceedingly heavy, particularly with the top growth, and can cause a barrier to the wind. If this growth is caught by a sudden gust, it can blow over and pull down the support with it.

One of the most satisfactory methods of fixing supporting wires is by vine eyes, protruding some 3–5cm (1.5–2in) from the wall and linked by galvanised or green plastic coated wire, both horizontally and vertically, to form a wide mesh. One can also buy wall nails which can be driven into the wall in between bricks, and to which wires can be attached either around the nail or through a hole provided at the end of the nail. There are several popular products available in the garden centre which are quite practical,

namely plastic hooks that are affixed in minutes using a super glue type of adhesive, and others that use a hardened steel nail driven through a hole in a plastic hook.

A well built wooden trellis is another well tried and successful means over which to train your climbing plant. The trellis should be coated with a wood preservative. Those that are bought from the garden centre may be coated in a brown material which is likely to be creosote. Freshly coated creosote will burn a plant, and therefore it is wise to leave your trellis in the elements for a year in order for it to weather. If you choose to make a trellis yourself from 2.5cm (1in) slats of sawn timber, it is worth remembering

23

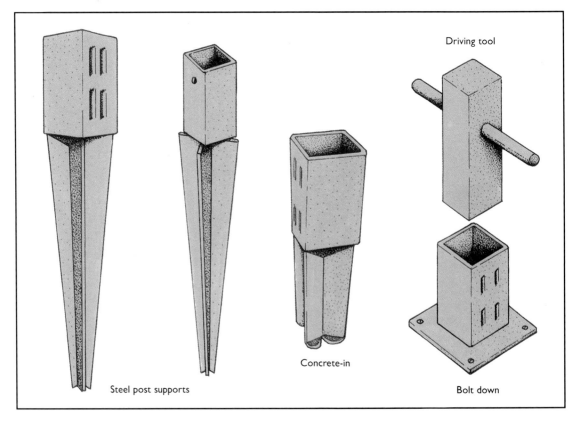

Fig 18   Fencing post supports of various proprietary makes help to make the task of fence and trellis erection a simple matter with satisfactory results.

to use galvanised nails which, because of their coating, have a prolonged life before rusting through.

Water soluble preservatives are becoming more common and are now available in a range of colours, from almost natural wood to dark brown, and through into a range of greens. These preservatives are quite harmless to plants and the trellis can therefore be used immediately after coating the wood. There are also various makes of excellent plastic netting now available with a mesh of 2.5sq cm (1sq in) and generally sold under the name of clematis netting. This can be purchased in rolls and when stretched between fixings, makes a very good support for climbing plants.

When fixing trellis to the wall, make sure that there is enough space between the trellis and the wall to allow the stems to twine comfortably and for you to place your ties of raffia or garden twine. Whatever your chosen means of support, be sure that it is strong enough to take the weight of climbers. I know that I am repeating this advice but it is important to realise that with the passing of time, this weight can become quite considerable. The top growth of climbers often hangs out above the trellis and this can be extensively buffeted in bad storms and, under extreme conditions, the complete plant and trellis can be pulled away from the wall. From experience, it is most difficult to re-fix such a trellis and invariably much damage is caused to the stems of the

Fig 19   An example of an arbour of brick and wood construction.

climber. Should you be so unfortunate, it is a wise move to cut the climber down by half or more, re-fix the trellis and await nature's healing powers to make good your losses.

NATURAL TENDENCIES

Most twining plants support themselves naturally and are therefore easy to grow. Those with a more vigorous habit need watching, for if they are allowed total freedom they can smother valuable shrubs. Thick trunks of trees are safe, they are less vulnerable, but it is the slender stemmed plants that a twining plant grasps more easily. Old trees, perhaps those that no longer fruit and flower, may be used as hosts for twining plants, but the shoots of the plant may have to be encouraged to twist around the branches and be held in place with soft twine or similar material. This means a lot of work

but the result is usually very attractive and worth the effort.

It is interesting to note that plants with twining stems do not always twine in the same way. Honeysuckle and the Hop twine clockwise, however, *Convolvulus* (bindweed) twines anti-clockwise. This is described in the well known Flanders and Swann song 'The Honeysuckle and the Bindweed'. It does not matter whether the plant is grown in the Northern Hemisphere or the Southern Hemisphere, it will still twine in its own inimitable way. Some climbing roses have thorns that point backwards to assist the upward growth. Some climbers have tendrils rather like fingers which curl and grip around the host support, such as *Clematis* and the pea family. The true vines are *Vitis* (the grape) and have lateral shoots and coil like tight springs around any near-by support. Thus the methods and devices used by plants to climb are very diverse.

25

However, the more fastidious of us might wish to contain the climber in a restricted space and will need to fight the natural habit of these 'hold fasts' by using readily available small wire loops, circles, raffia or soft twine. Also available are 'twist-ems', a simple device of a narrow, plastic sheathed flexible wire which can encircle the training wire and the climbing shoots, the circle being completed by twisting the two ends. It is well to realise that it is not good policy to tie these loops too tightly as some climbing shoots are very soft and delicate when young and can grow larger and more woody as the climber ages.

OTHER STRUCTURES

Whether your garden is bounded by wall, fence or hedge, it is pleasing to be able to soften such structures. A wall is a precious adjunct to a garden no matter which way it faces. Some walls are so old and beautiful that it would be a sad thing to cover them completely with climbing plants. Some brickwork or stonework should show through here and there.

Fences, on the contrary, can be completely covered. It is wise not to plant climbers against fence posts but to plant them between the uprights. Should the fence need repair at some

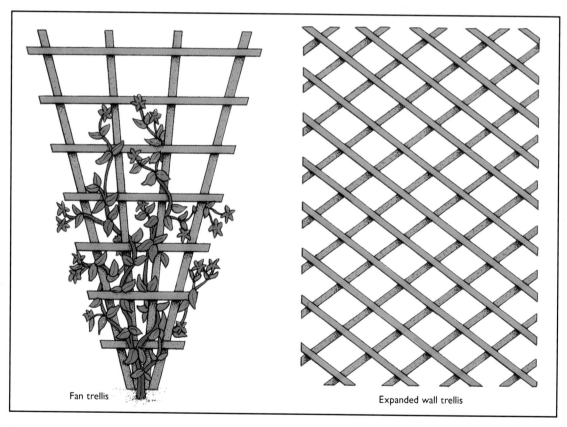

Fan trellis

Expanded wall trellis

Fig 20   Two sorts of modern trellis. These should be attached to the wall using vine eyes or wall nails. They will give another opportunity to grow climbing plants, particularly those with variegated foliage and are an excellent support for sweet peas and nasturtiums.

*Fig 21   A delightful treatment for a pathway using various sized stones,
the path leading through an archway to a different part of the garden.*

stage, it is invariably to the posts that attention is
needed. Fences are seldom used other than as
boundaries and as such, whatever the support, it
must be firm and long lasting. Nothing is more in-
furiating than having achieved a good screen, to
have the support collapse.

Concrete posts with fencing panels and stout
wires between them will prove long lasting as a
support. In cold districts, tying plants tightly to
wire can damage all but the hardiest and
therefore insulated wire should be used. Some
climbing plants are self supporting but still need a
little guidance when young and newly planted.
Ivies are a good example, as are *Hydrangea
petiolaris*, the *Vitis* species and the attractive
Parthenocissus.

For all-year-round clothing of your garden
structures, choose plants that do not shed their
leaves. Again, ivies are ideal, some take on lovely

winter colours and the variegated species are
always most attractive. They both flower and
fruit, and birds and bees are very grateful for this
harvest. *Pyracantha* species are hardy, and they
too have flowers and berries and can be clipped
into shape. If you already have a dark green yew
or holly hedge, do try to grow one of the
vigorous climbers through it, such as *Clematis
montana* or *Tropaeolum speciosum*. The effect
of the lighter flowers growing through the dark
background is quite dramatic.

Whereas shrubs can be trained horizontally at
the base and so keep a screen solid to the
ground, most climbers are apt to grow upwards
with the result that they tend not only to be bare
at the base but coarse and overpowering at the
top. It is recommended to plant a dwarf shrub to
fill in the lower part of the screen. It could be an
evergreen or a shrub that will contrast and

27

Fig 22   A selection of modern fences. These are often used to make
boundaries or internal divisions within a garden. They are ideal structures for
supporting climbing plants, providing they are erected securely and solidly, as
the weight of plant material can eventually become quite considerable.

Fig 24   An example of trompe l'oeil, *achieved by using trellis and a central mirror on an end wall or fence. Delicate climbers woven into the trellis enhances the whole effect. The mirror should be used unobtrusively with the edges well hidden making the difference between illusion and reality difficult to detect.*

Fig 23   An example of trompe l'oeil.

complement the climbing plant, one that will flower or produce its special foliage at the same time as the climbing plant or at a different season. This will cover the bare stems of the climber and add further interest to the planting.

If it is a feasible proposition, consider a planted tunnel. This can be made with hoops of metal, as large as space will allow. These should be set at regular intervals over a path and linked with spars of the same material. The climbing plants should be trained in an upwards direction and the branches trained along. Grape vines are ideal for this purpose as are *Wisteria* and *Laburnum*.

A simple gate in low walls can look rather fussy.

In order to give them stature and emphasise their importance as a barrier to be crossed before entering a new area of the garden, they can be topped with an archway of trellis or welded iron to support climbing plants. This offers a secure structure, particularly if attached to steel posts, and is a good support for quick growing evergreen climbers which will rapidly conceal the man-made look. In tiny gardens, the *trompe l'oeil* effect of outdoor mirror glass set into trellis work can deceive one's perception of the actual size of the garden very effectively. Evidence from sculpture and paintings has also given us the idea of twining stems of climbing plants around ropes hanging in loose swags. Ropes or chains hang down in curves from the tops of tall poles fixed into the ground. Plants are encouraged to climb up the columns and along the swags. Ivy is particularly effective if used in this way and has the advantage of being evergreen.

29

CHAPTER 6

Recommended Climbing Plants and Wall Shrubs

I have chosen those that I believe to be the best and readily available in either specialist nurseries or garden centres.

ABELIA *Caprifoliaceae*

A. x grandiflora A splendid wall plant that does well at the base of a south or west wall. It has white or pink, slightly fragrant, bell-shaped flowers which are borne in twos and threes in the leaf axils. The leaves are light green and the flowers bloom from July to October. This is ever popular with bees gathering late season honey.

Abelias grow to 1–1.5m (3.3–5ft) and have brown, slightly arching stems which need to be tied in to training wires or trellis. They are partially evergreen.

Cultural Notes Pruning is restricted to keeping the plant within bounds and cutting out the older wood, in order to encourage new growth. Prune in spring. Cuttings of semi-ripe wood strike easily.

A. x grandiflora 'Frances Mason' For foliage colour, look for 'Frances Mason' which has golden yellow flushed variegated leaves and bears pink flowers. There is also a recently introduced clone called 'Gold Strike' which has almost pure gold leaves.

ABELIOPHYLLUM *Oleaceae*

A. distichum Korea. A delicately scented white flowering shrub whose flowers appear in February on bare twigs and are a pleasure to see so early in the year. It seems to be rarely offered by specialist nurseries and indeed, it is doubtful whether it is stocked by most garden centres. It flowers best after a hot summer and needs to be planted near a sunny south wall. This is a slow growing shrub.

Cultural Notes Prune only to cut out any weak or dead wood. Propagate by cuttings taken in summer of half ripe wood.

ABUTILON *Malvaceae* (Mallow)

There are several species of mallow that can be grown in England in the shelter of a wall. Most are rather tall growing and are more usually seen in their variegated form. This variegation is a transmissible virus leaf condition and these plants are, in the main, used as annual bedding plants or specimen plants. They are not totally hardy in severe winters.

A. megapotamicum This is an excellent low shrub for south facing walls and usually makes 1–1.5m (3.3–5ft) of growth in a season. It has light green, long pointed leaves. From May till autumn, the flowers are the attraction for they

30

Fig 25   Abutilon megapotamicum *in flower.*

are large compared to the slender growths and the narrow, pointed leaves. The flowers are pendulous with round red calyces and contrasting yellow petals and a central boss of rich brown stamens. Young plants are susceptible to frost damage and should be protected.

A. megapotamicum 'Variegatum'   This has leaves irregularly splashed with yellow. This variegation is virus induced and the patterning of the leaves certainly draws the attention.

Cultural Notes   Tie in the slender growths and treat as a climber. I would be surprised if it needed any pruning for, in my experience, winter frosts do the job for me.

ACANTHOPANAX *Araliaceae*

Although without floral attraction, the foliage is handsome with leaves of a compound character and of a type not usually seen in other plants. These leaves are deciduous, alternate, long stalked and usually consist of 3–7 leaflets.

A. sieboldianus   This is a deciduous shrub of loose growth habit, 20–30cm (8–11in) high with erect stems and slender, arching branches with a spine at the base of each leaf stalk or leaf cluster. Coming from China and Japan, for many years gardeners confined it to a cool greenhouse. However, I am convinced that it is quite hardy if given shelter from north and east winds and trained to wires affixed to a wall.

A. s. 'Variegatus'   This cultivar has leaflets edged with a border of creamy-white and is one of the daintiest of variegated shrubs. I would be quite lost without one of these shrubs somewhere in my garden. The annual growths must be tied back to wires but, because of its spines, one should take care when handling.

31

Cultural Notes   Prune back in early spring to fill the alloted space before growth commences.

ACONITUM *Ranunculaceae*
(Monkshood)

A. bulleyanum   This is an herbaceous perennial climber and is one of 300 north temperate species. It is readily distinguished by the helmet-like sepal at the top of each blue-purple flower which is often a loose, drooping raceme, hence the common name of Monkshood. It is best climbing through a tallish spring flowering shrub to provide colour and interest when the shrub has given its best display. This plant requires a moisture retentive fertile soil in sun or partial shade and it blooms from August to late autumn, weather permitting.

Cultural Notes   Young growth is particularly prone to slug damage. Use slug pellets every spring as a precaution. Cut down the flowering stems in October.

ACTINIDIA *Actinidiaceae*
(Chinese gooseberry)

A genus of over forty deciduous hardy twining climbers from Eastern Asia with plants of interesting foliage, flowers and fruit. Suitable in any fertile soil and a partially shaded and sheltered site.

A. chinensis   This is best known for its fruits, Chinese gooseberries, now known as Kiwi fruits. It grows to 10m (33ft) or more and the young stems are coated with conspicuous red hairs. These red hairs set off the rounded dark green foliage. The 4cm (1.5in) wide flowers are white on opening, gradually maturing to creamy-buff. While hermaphrodite plants are known, both sexes of this plant are needed for fruit production and for this purpose, the plant is best grown in full sun. This is not a plant to be grown in the north of England as it is not entirely hardy in all areas.

A. kolomikta (Cat plant)   This plant also comes from China, Korea and Japan and is my choice of climber for a sunny wall. When it is at its best in good sunlight, it is a show stopper, for the heart-shaped leaves change most dramatically to half green, half white, flushed with pink. This colouring can cover just the tips or the whole leaf. Later in the season, the colour fades. It is believed that male plants are more common in gardens and that they colour better than those of the female. Unlike *A. chinensis*, *A. kolomikta* is rather more bushy and in gardens, usually climbs to 3–4m (10–13ft). The flowers are small, fragrant and white but are usually hidden by the leaves.

Cultural Notes   A little gentle pruning to keep the plant within its allotted space and well furnished is recommended by shortening leading growths and so maintaining a good clothing of the wall. This should be carried out early in the year before leaf emergence. It is wise to protect the base of your plant with wire netting from the nibbling and frantic rubbing activities of cats which can injure a young plant.

A. polygama   This plant is also tolerably hardy in England and is suitable for a sunny wall. It is known as the Silver Vine as it has silvery-white variegated leaves, similar to *A. kolomikta*. It is not as tender as *A. chinensis*. As in the case of *A. kolomikta*, it is the male plants that have the silvery leaves whilst the female have only green. Unfortunately, this is rarely offered in the trade in this country.

ADLUMIA *Fumariaceae*
(Climbing fumitory)

A. fungosa   Although in its native country this is a biennial, it is, to all intents and purposes in southern England, only suitable for scrambling up a tall shrub. It has slender stems growing to 3–4m (10–13ft) with fern-like dissected leaves which cling to their support. The flowers are white to pinky-mauve in sizeable panicles from late summer to autumn. The plant resents wind and is best in dappled sunshine. At best, this is a curiosity as the flowers are pale and somewhat insipid in colour.

Cultural Notes   This plant is grown from seed as soon as ripe. The seedlings should be pricked off into pots or directly into the site. There is a need to prevent root damage in the first year. Plants form neat rosettes with the climbing stems following in the second year.

AKEBIA *Lardizabalaceae*
(Chocolate Vine)

Eastern USA. Both species are hardy in England and are either deciduous or semi-evergreen with compound leaves composed of either 3 or 5 radiating leaflets. This is a most vigorous and decorative species.

A. quinata   This is probably the most commonly grown of the two species. It is best suited to clothe an unsightly shed, twining over a fence that has been furnished with training wires or can be useful to cover an old tree. Its leaves are a soft green and in spring flushed with purple. The flowers, hidden amongst the leaves, are small strings of a pale green colour. By late spring, these buds become chocolate to maroon-purple and are spicily fragrant.

Cultural Notes   Both species are readily propagated by hardwood and semi-hardwood cuttings. Seeds can be sown when ripe or in the spring. When the fruits are ripe, they split to reveal black seeds on the white inside pulp. From my experience, when attention is drawn to the flowers, there is always excited comment, both for the exquisite formation of the flowers and the exciting spicy fragrance.

  Only rarely has my plant given me the bonus of the bright purple sausage-like fruits. It is possible that in England, it requires a mild spring and a hot summer to produce these startling fruits.

A. trifoliata   This plant is equally vigorous and fully deciduous. The flowers are, if anything,

Fig 26   A climbing plant will soon cover an unsightly tree stump.

smaller than the preceding species. However, the purple fruits are anything up to 12cm (4.5in) long and 4–6cm (1.5–2in) wide and are thus even more striking.

AMPELOPSIS *Vitaceae*

Asia and North America. These plants were originally classified along with the Grape Vine, genus *Vitis*. All the *Ampelopsis* have curly tendrils by which they can, with initial support, climb trees and fences. They do not have self-clinging pads by which to cover walls without assistance. All are deciduous. The Virginia Creeper should be referred to under *Parthenocissus*, but in older books and catalogues, *Ampelopsis* were classified under *Vitis*.

A. aconitifolia   This plant has fine leaflets which are deeply divided giving an airy and fern-like

33

appearance. This is possibly the most elegant of the species. The tiny green flowers open in late summer, followed by small orange to yellow fruits.

A. brevipedunculata (A. heterophylla) This plant can clothe a wall or pergola to perfection. The main pleasure that this plant gives over and above its clothing capacity is that in a hot summer, it bears bright blue fruits.

***A. brevipedunculata* 'Elegans' (*A.b.* 'Variegata', *A.b.* 'Tricolour', *A.b. heterophylla* 'Variegata')** This is a weaker growing and slightly tender plant. However, it has superior white and pink mottled, somewhat distorted leaves. This is often grown as a pot plant in a tub and given shelter from the cold of winter in a cold greenhouse. I enjoy growing it at the foot of a south facing wall in the shelter of, and at the foot of, two evergreen shrubs. This too, in a good summer, has wonderful blue fruits but I am gardening in the south of England. For those in the north, try the pot method. In full sun, there is some scorching of the white and pink splashed leaves. For this reason, perhaps it is best on an east facing wall.

A. megalophylla This has the distinction of the largest leaves of any vine, 45–60cm (17–23in) long. The ovate toothed leaves are rich green above and glaucous beneath. The plant climbs to 8–9m (26–29ft) but is a slow grower and can be used to great effect trained over an arbour or to cover a tall wall or fence.

Cultural Notes Easily propagated by half-ripened wood growths taken in July or August.

ARISTOLOCHIA Aristolochiaceae (Dutchman's pipe)

Mainly of tropical origin with no less than 300 species spread around the world. They are mainly woody, climbing twiners, both evergreen and deciduous. The flowers are interesting in that there is no corolla but the tubular calyx is bent in

Fig 27   A climber trained against a conventional pattern of crossed wires.

shape so that it resembles a Dutch smoking pipe. The calyx is flared, forming the bowl and gives the impression of a petal.

A. macrophylla The flowers appear in summer and are more or less obscured by the leaves. It is deciduous and hardy, growing to 8m (26ft) or more and effectively covers a wall or pergola. The Dutchman's pipe-like small flowers have yellow-green, U-shaped tubes and brown-purple 3-lobed purple bowls.

AZARA Flacourtiaceae

Chile and Argentina. These plants are suspect hardy in all but the most favourable conditions in the south of England.

A. microphylla Grown as an evergreen wall shrub, this has the most wonderful vanilla fragrance emanating from its insignificant yellow-green flowers which are borne in profusion in

February from the undersides of the stems. The leaves are small and holly-like and are a brilliant green.

***A. microphylla* 'Variegata'**   This is the variegated form of *A. microphylla* with white-edged leaves.

BERBERIDOPSIS Flacourtiaceae
(Coral plant)

B. corallina   Chile. This is a plant for connoisseurs and is an evergreen twiner 2–3m (7–10ft) in height with rich green foliage. It needs a deep, moist soil and shade with protection from winds. Suitable for a north wall, it will need some support and can be trained to scramble over a host shrub. It has pendant trusses of crimson flowers during the summer and autumn.

Cultural Notes   Can be propagated easily from layers or cuttings at any time of the year.

BERCHEMIA Rhamnaceae

B. racemosa   Japan. Unfortunately, its chief attraction is the rich black fruits and these are rarely, if ever, produced in Britain. The greenish flowers are small and insignificant. It is a strong growing scandent shrub rather than a climber. Grows well in a good moist soil but could be tender in the north of England and needing winter protection.

***B. racemosa* 'Variegata'**   I have grown this variegated form with some success against a wall and have seen it growing in Winchester in a similar position but, in each case, the plants were 2–3 years old and well established in pots in greenhouses and thoroughly hardened off before planting out.

BILLARDIERA Pittosporaceae

Australia and Tasmania. This plant needs a rich humus, neutral to acid soil and thrives in sun or partial shade.

B. longifolia   This can be grown from seeds in spring or cuttings in late summer. Excellent rambling through a wall shrub. The leaves are 3–5cm (1–2in) long and are elliptic to lanceolate. From the axils of the leaves, dangle solitary 3cm (1in) long greenish-yellow bells. Berries follow, varying in colour, curiously, from plant to plant from deep blue to shades of purple, white or red. In the south of England, it is best grown on a south facing wall. In the north, treat as a coldhouse climber, just needing frost protection and kept just above freezing point.

BOMAREA Alstromeriaceae

South America. There are as many as 150 species and this genus needs the attention of the taxonomist. It is closely related to *Alstromeria*, the Peruvian lily.

B. caldasii   This plant is recommended as it climbs up to 3–4m (10–13ft) and is a handsome, half hardy plant presenting a challenge to the connoisseur grower. The flowers are yellow, flushed orange, or wholly orange or red with greenish-brown spotting on the inner petals. I have grown it out of doors, in Hertfordshire for two to three years from plants started from seed. It has flowered well for me as it makes very deep rooted fattened tuberous roots which need some winter protection such as bracken, straw or mounds of leaf litter. However, one extreme cold winter put paid to the pleasure of its twining stems and gorgeous flowers. Recently, I had the pleasure of seeing in Cheshire, a most wonderful arbour completely covered with its climbing and twining growths and the bell-like flowers hanging down beneath the leaf axils. True, the site was a perfect micro-climate between walls and hedges, ideal for half-hardy subjects.

BOUGAINVILLEA Nyctaginaceae

It is such a pity that we cannot grow examples of this genus out of doors unless, of course, one is situated in an ideal micro-climate in the south of

England, but it does make an ideal climbing wall plant in a cold greenhouse, kept just above freezing. With the present trend to sun lounges and garden rooms and with care, one should be able to grow this plant by providing a small flower bed in the floor of such a room. The bracts are the parts of the plant that provide the colour and this display can be a vivid magenta, coppery-orange, pink, white, scarlet or crimson. There is a clone that has leaves boldly marked with white and this makes a splendid foliage plant.

B. 'Sanderiana' This is extremely floriferous and is one of the best for pot culture.

B. 'Surprise' This has bracts that can be all white, all rose or a mixture of the two. Naturally, this looks quite dramatic.

CALYSTEGIA Convolvulaceae (Bindweed)

Of over twenty species, all are invasive and some almost impossible to eradicate. They are closely allied to the common bindweed. Most gardeners have, at some time, tried to rid their garden of this plant which undoubtedly has most attractive funnel-shaped trumpet flowers.

C. japonica For those who would like to try a *Calystegia*, seek out *C. japonica*. It climbs to 5m (16ft) or more and has narrow, arrow-shaped leaves and most attractive rich pink flowers which are about 5cm (2in) long.

C. japonica 'Flore-pleno' This is yet another attractive flowering form. It has sterile double flowers, flesh pink in colour which tend to darken to bright rose. The petals are long and wavy.

Cultural Notes Can be grown in all ordinary soils either in sun or partial shade. Both forms can be increased by root division or root cuttings. The roots are deeply delving with slender rhizomes. It is best planted in a bottomless plastic bucket sunk into the ground so that if it escapes

this restriction, it will not be too difficult to dig out the errant roots and keep it within bounds.

CAMPSIS Bignoniaceae (Trumpet Vine)

China, South-east USA. Both species mentioned are hardy in Britain but need the shelter of a south wall with ample sun to flower effectively.

C. radicans This is the hardier of the two listed here. A showy, deciduous self-clinging climber with pinnate foliage. The leaves are dark green above and downy beneath. The flowers are trumpet shaped and of a glorious orange-scarlet colour produced in August onwards on the ends of the current season's growth. There is a yellow form *C. radicans* 'Flava' which should be sought from specialist nurseries.

C. grandiflora This is a non-clinging species and needs 'tying in' to the framework of wire or trellis. It only flowers well in this country during long hot summers. The flowers are perhaps even more attractive than the previous species in that they are larger with the throat of the flower orange with yellow-orange flared lobes.

Cultural Notes Once the framework of stems of the annual growth have reached their allotted space, prune back after leaf fall to 2–3 buds on the previous season's growth. Propagation is by cuttings or layering.

CELASTRUS Celastraceae

North-east Asia. A vigorous twining climber but with flowers of little interest. However, the pea-sized fruits split open to reveal vivid scarlet seeds within yellow husks. These fruits hang in chains and make a splendid display lasting for quite some time as apparently, birds do not seem to be interested in these seeds.

C. orbiculatus refers to the shape of rounded 5cm (2in) long leaves which turn yellow in autumn and so are a perfect foil for the show of hanging fruits. In order to enjoy this display of fruits and seeds, it is necessary to purchase a male and a female plant and grow them side by side. However, there is a hermaphrodite form having both male and female flowers on the one plant but this would have to be sought from a specialist nursery.

Cultural Notes   Grows well in ordinary soil in sun or partial shade. Propagation is by layering.

CESTRUM Solanaceae

C. newellii   Central America. Although this is really a wall shrub, it is worth trying if one is living in the south of England. Its funnel-shaped, bright red flowers are borne in clusters and are most attractive. Seek this out from a specialist nursery.

C. elegans   Evergreen, and with flowers more purple than those of the above. This plant succeeds well in Cornwall against a sheltered wall. I remember seeing it in flower at Hilliers of Winchester on an east wall. I was told that it had endured up to twenty degrees of frost.

CHAENOMELES Rosaceae
(Japonica)

This deciduous and hardy shrub is the well known japonica, or ornamental quince. It is usually seen grown on walls and trained to cover its allotted space by being tied in to wires or trellis. The flowers are produced from March onwards and there are several species and many hybrids all with different colours of flowers. Plants will often bear fruit which can be made into excellent quince jelly. Look out for 'Cardinalis' with crimson scarlet flowers, 'Moerloosii' with white or pink flowers, 'Nivalis' with pure white and a compact growing form, 'Simonii' with dark crimson flowers. The brilliant red flowered 'Knap Hill Scarlet' can be readily found in garden centres and nurseries as probably can the above named varieties.

Cultural Notes   Requires a modicum of pruning to shorten the spurs to 2–3 buds after flowering. Any dead wood should be cut out.

CHIMONANTHUS
Calycanthaceae (Wintersweet)

C. praecox   China. The common name is very apt for it flowers in the depth of winter on bare twigs and is wonderfully perfumed. It is a perfectly hardy deciduous shrub in the open ground but is more frequently grown as a wall plant and as such, the flowers appear somewhat earlier. When well trained, one is able to appreciate and examine the flowers closely. These are 2–3cm (0.5–1in) in length, the outer petals are a greenish yellow and the inner ones purplish in colour. The pointed, bright green leaves are 7–10cm (2.8–4in) long and half as wide and have a rough upper surface. In some years, light green flask-shaped fruits are an added attraction. Although incorrect, this plant is often listed in nurseries under *Chimonanthus fragrans*.

Cultural Notes   Prune back to its allotted space. It is a notably difficult plant to propagate but can be layered with some success.

CHOISYA Rutaceae
(Mexican Orange Blossom)

C. ternata   South America. This is an evergreen shrub that needs plenty of sun and protection from cold east winds. The flowers in early spring are white and fragrant and are borne on the previous year's growth. It grows vigorously in any soil and makes a rounded bush, 1–5m (3.3–16ft) high by as much across. It really is worth including in this list for the fragrance of its flowers and while there is a dearth of such perfume in the garden at that time of year.

C. ternata 'Sundance'   This is a new clone selected within the last few years. It has leaves of a glorious golden yellow. It is a little slower growing and as such is ideal for the smaller garden, and can be used as a focal point against darker green leaves.

Cultural Notes   Can readily be pruned back after flowering. New growth will break from older wood.

CLEMATIS Ranunculaceae

As there are so many superb Clematis, I have devoted an entire section to this genus. (See pages 80–93).

CLIANTHUS Leguminosae
(Parrot's bill or Lobster claw)

C. puniceus   New Zealand. Although this is a shrub and not a climber, it is included here as I feel it is highly desirable for its flowers. It is worth taking a little effort to protect it, particularly in the north of England during very cold winters. It is a thin stemmed shrub and can reach 2–3m (7–10ft) or more trained on a south or west facing wall and should be planted in a well drained soil. The bright red flowers resemble a lobster's claw and appear during June and July. It is evergreen with light green pinnate leaves.

Cultural Notes   In all but the mildest areas in the south, it is wise to cover in winter with straw, bracken or a large polythene sheet hung from the wall and stretched down to soil level and then pegged into the ground. Propagation is by cuttings taken during the summer.

COBAEA Cobaeaceae

C. scandens   South America. In its native country this is a perennial, but in England it is treated as an annual. (See Annual Climbers, page 114).

CODONOPSIS Campanulaceae
(Bonnet bellflower)

Asia. This is an herbaceous climber. The simple leaves are alternate and the flowers usually

Fig 28   Campanula grown in a pot, set into a wall niche and grown as a trailing plant.

terminal, nodding and much like those of a Campanula. It needs sun and an ordinary moisture retentive soil. The roots are fattened and are variously tuber-like. The climber can reach to 2m (6.5ft) or more, the stems are very slender and when it flowers in late summer, holds clusters of blooms that are amazingly wide of about 5cm (2in) in size and these will open out flat to five lobes. These are violet-blue and there are other colour forms. In my experience, it is best in a sheltered site with its growth in the sun and roaming through a shrub.

C. vinciflora, C. viridiflora   The former has purple to lilac blue flowers and the latter has green flowers with a patterning of purple on the inside of the bell.

C. clematidea   This has nodding bells of a pale, cloudy blue, beautifully marked with maroon rings inside the bell. Some observers can detect a fox-like aroma rather like that experienced when standing close to *Fritillaria imperialis*.

CONVOLVULUS *Convolvulaceae*

This is a widespread and large genus of over 200 species and contains annuals, perennials and shrubs. The three species described here need a well-drained soil and a sheltered sunny site.

C. althaeoides   This comes from the Mediterranean region and trails and twines, depending on available support. First growth in the season seems to lie flat on the ground but this eventually climbs up to about 1m (3.3ft) to gain as much sun and warmth as it can. The grey-green leaves are ovate with the basal ones shallowly lobed, the upper leaves are deeply pedate. From late summer, the upper leaf axils bear 1–3 very wide cone-shaped rosy pink flowers, each 2–3cm (0.5–1in) across.

C. elegantissimus *(Syn. mauritanicus)*   Also from the Mediterranean but whose leaves are coated with silky silvery hairs and it has solitary flowers. It looks best scrambling over a low shrub. It is prostrate at first, then twining and is perennial. It has blue flowers about 2cm (0.5in) across. Both these species can be invasive and it is recommended that their roots are contained from wandering too far by using slates inserted vertically around their roots. I have found that they eventually escape and wander far and wide. As they are not totally hardy, any excess of exuberant growth has been curbed by the two extreme cold winters that we have had in the last fifteen years. I now plant them for safety, each in a very large deep trough which resembles a miniature rock garden and these are situated on a terrace in a favoured sunny sheltered position.

Cultural Notes   Propagated by division, by cuttings in sand in August or by seed.

C. cneorum   This is a low-growing shrub with lovely felted silver leaves which makes a good foil for the white and blush pink funnel-shaped flowers in summer. It grows well in a chalky soil but needs a sheltered spot in full sun with good drainage. I would not like to be without this plant in my garden. In the north, it might be prudent to plant it at the foot of a south facing wall and providing that there is good drainage, this could well be under the overhang of the house eaves. Do remember to give the plant water every so often in summer if it is in such a position.

CORONILLA *Leguminaceae*

Southern Europe. **C. glauca**   An evergreen shrub, usually too tender to be grown fully in the open but can be in many counties in the south of England if planted in a sunny sheltered spot against a wall to show off its yellow pea-like flowers and is most attractive when flowering. The leaves are glaucous, light green and very delicate.

There is a variegated form, *Coronilla glauca variegata* which unfortunately, I have discovered is more tender than the normal green leaved form. I now grow it as a tub plant which is consigned to a frost-free cold greenhouse for the winter months.

Cultural Notes   Light pruning keeps the plant within bounds. Readily propagated from the fully ripened wood.

COTONEASTER *Rosaceae*

C. horizontalis   China. A wonderful, totally hardy shrub which, when planted at the foot of almost any wall, in sun or shade, grows horizontally but can be trained upwards to great effect. This enables it to display the herring-bone habit of growth. The flowers are small, white flushed with pink. Its glossy, dark green leaves are 0.5cm (0.2in) or so long and are a roundish oval with the apex quite pointed. The foliage begins to fade in November and dies off gradually into shades of orange and red. This combined with the prolific red berries during autumn and winter can be a truly magnificent sight.

If you are wishing to clothe a wall to any great height, the main stems should be tied in, lest snow and wind spoil your endeavours.

There is a variegated form, *C.h.* 'Variegata' of which there seem to be two clones in circulation at the moment. Look for the clone that has a wider band of creamy white as against the one with a narrower band which is not so dramatic against the green.

C. microphylla An evergreen, low growing shrub, spreading to a width of 3m (10ft) or more. The leaves are ovate, 0.5–0.75cm (0.2–0.5in) long and are a very deep shining green, grey and downy beneath. This is most suitable for growing up and over dwarf walls of, say, under 1m (3.3ft) and it will completely envelop the wall, hugging its contours. If you are fortunate enough to have a dwarf wall with earth between its construction over a raised bed, this is an ideal shrub to trail and allowed to hang down. This can be a fabulous sight for flower and berry. To my mind, this is Nature's architecture at its best.

Cultural Notes Can be readily pruned to keep the plant within bounds. Easily propagated by seed or cuttings of semi-ripened wood which should be taken in August.

CRINODENDRON
Elaeocarpaceae

C. hookerianum Chile. A most attractive evergreen shrub needing, in all but the mildest parts of England, the advantage of a warm wall, but out of hot sun. Flowers in early summer. It produces urn-shaped fleshy flowers of a rich red and these contrast with the deep green lance-shaped leaves. Apart from its need for warmth, a neutral or lime free soil will help this shrub to give of its best.

Cultural Notes Can be pruned to keep in shape and to remove dead wood.

CYTISUS Leguminosae (Broom)

This deciduous shrub is reasonably hardy in Britain and is usually grown in the north as a wall shrub and tied in as required because of its lax growth habit.

C. battandieri The trifoliate leaves with leaflets 3–7cm (1.25in) long are covered in silky, silvery hairs and are a perfect foil for the fragrant, rich yellow flowers which have a pineapple scent and are of typical Broom appearance. These flowers are borne in clusters at the end of the young leafy shoots.

Cultural Notes This shrub does not need pruning unless there is dead wood to be removed. Usually raised from seed but seedlings may take a number of years before flowering.

DECUMARIA Hydrangeaceae

D. sinensis China. A woody evergreen climber related to the Hydrangea. This has ovate, lustrous yellow-green leaves up to 9cm (3.5in) long and bears cream, honey scented flowers in summer. This is an uncommon and pleasing wall cover and should at least be tried if you can find a nursery that offers it. Site in sheltered half shade.

Cultural Notes Propagated by cuttings in late summer.

DESFONTAINEA Potaliaceae

D. spinosa Chile. A most unusual and beautiful looking plant. Its leaves look much like those of holly. However, the dark green leaves are opposite, and not alternate like those of holly. When the plant is in flower, it is festooned with scarlet-red and yellow funnel-shaped flowers which have five yellow lobes and are about 4cm (1.5in) long and just over 1cm (0.2in) wide. The flowers are produced from July to September from the leaf axils and look really well against the dark green of the holly-like leaves. It enjoys a moist, frost-free climate such as that in the west coast of Scotland. However, I have seen it in varying situations, always flowering well. A wall, somewhat shaded and facing south-west suits it best.

Cultural Notes   The cherry-like fruits contain small black seeds from which this plant is propagated. It is notoriously difficult to propagate from cuttings.

DICHELOSTEMMA Alliaceae

D. volubilis   North-west America. An unusual climber for it grows from a corm and has grass-like leaves. Its pink, starry to bell-shaped flowers are borne in summer on long twining stems. A light, well drained soil, with sun and frost protection is needed in all but the very mildest parts of Britain.

ECCREMOCARPUS Bignoniaceae
(Chilean Glory Flower)

E. scaber   Chile. A woody perennial, growing to 3m (10ft) or more. In hard winters it can be cut down to ground level but will often shoot from the base in the spring. The normal colour form of the flowers is orange; they are bottle-shaped and hang in racemes.

There are two interesting colour forms of flower, *E. aureus* with yellow flowers and *E. carmineus* with carmine-red flowers. All flower from summer to late autumn. The plant climbs by the branched tendrils produced by the pinnate leaves. A warm wall suits it best in the colder parts of Britain. I have seen all three colour forms of this plant growing against a 3m (10ft) high sunny, red brick wall. True, it was in a Jersey garden and in August. There must have been many thousands of bottle-shaped flowers hanging down from the plants, starting from midway up the wall. This was a sight I shall never forget. I obtained seed from this planting and, fifteen years later, I am still saving and sowing

Fig 29   Eccremocarpus scaber.

seed and enjoying it every year. I gather seed as an insurance policy should we have a hard winter. It is interesting to realise that my plants today are direct descendants from those that I gathered while on that Jersey holiday. Many of my friends too have enjoyed the bounty of seed that these colour forms have produced.

Cultural Notes   It can be readily propagated from seed and from one seed pod can be raised many hundreds of plants. Sow the seeds early in spring with a little bottom heat, and then harden off before planting out in the garden in groupings of 2–3 plants.

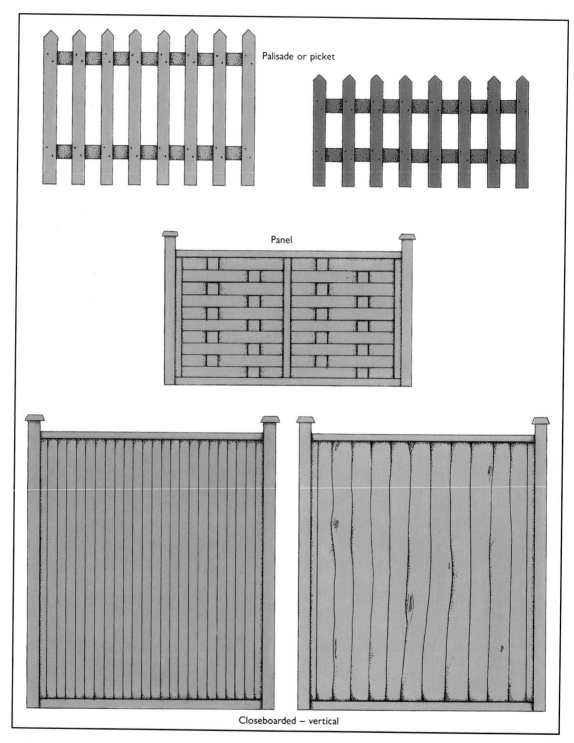

Fig 30   Modern forms of fencing. The palisade or picket fence is
particularly suitable for plants which climb by twining around their
support.

ELEAGNUS *Eleagnaceae*

E. glabra Japan and Central China. Not normally known as a climbing plant, this evergreen has a rambling habit and is used quite often on the Continent, especially in the warmer areas of Europe. It is used to cover sheds and walls of buildings which are made more attractive by the glossy, dark green foliage.

The leaves are 5–7cm (2–3in) long, and the lower surface is brown and shining with a metallic lustre. The white flowers are rather inconspicuous but very fragrant and open in October and November.

EUONYMUS *Celastraceae*

E. fortuneii var. radicans Japan. It is used particularly in Europe as a climber to grow up house walls. It can be seen in England completely covering the front walls of small terraced houses with the growth around the window apertures neatly clipped back. It climbs much in the manner of ivy and has elliptic to ovate alternate pairs of glossy green leaves. There are variegated forms of which there are several clones but *E.f.r.* 'Colorata', a green leaved form, takes on rich shades of red and purple in winter.

Cultural Notes Propagate by taking cuttings in summer or autumn.

FATSIA *Araliaceae*

F. japonica Japan. Whilst this is not a climber but a shrub, its large, divided palmate leaves can give your garden a lush, semi-tropical appearance. It will grow well in the climate of the south of England. Elsewhere, the plant should be given protection and a slightly shady position and is hardy in most of Britain. It will grow to about 2m (6.5ft) high and bears creamy white flowers. There is a variegated form where the leaves are splashed with white-cream but in my experience, it is slightly more tender but certainly an eye-catcher for the beauty of its leaves.

Cultural Notes Any soil seems to suit this plant and it will not require pruning unless its growth becomes too prolific.

FEIJOA *Myrtaceae*

F. sellowiana South America. A most unusual wall shrub. Like so many shrubs from South America, it can be grown in the warmer parts of Britain and is therefore best against a wall. It makes a rounded bush or small tree of 2×2m (6.5×6.5ft). Leaves are opposite and 1.5–5cm (0.6–2in) long, the undersides are felted which make an excellent foil for the most attractive flowers which have prominent long red stamens. There is a variegated form, *F. s. variegata* with white edged leaves. Unfortunately, fruit is seldom produced in this country when grown out of doors. I have eaten the fruit when in the Mediterranean area and our local supermarket offered it one year. The taste is most difficult to describe, it looks a little like a guava and has a distinct scented flavour. The petals are known to be edible and are pleasantly sweet. It is a plant worth trying in a sheltered spot. It does well at Kew and I saw it flowering against a wooden office hut at the old nurseries of Hilliers of Winchester some years ago.

Cultural Notes Pruning should be undertaken as soon as the flowering season is over. Remove the more outstanding growths so that the plant is kept reasonably close to the wall. Propagated by cuttings of half ripened wood with bottom heat.

FICUS *Moraceae* (Climbing Fig)

Far East. Whilst this is an evergreen climber suitable for walls, out of doors, in the milder climates, the pleasure of it to my mind is that it will grow in tolerably dense shade and looks quite attractive if one obtains the variegated form, *F. pumila* 'Variegata' which has white edged leaves which are heart-shaped, 1cm (0.2in) long and half as wide. It climbs like an ivy with adhering rootlets and is scarcely stalked and lies flattened against a wall. It can climb up to 10m (33ft) in favourable conditions.

Cultural Notes Any well drained soil is suitable. Mature branches should be clipped to shape. Propagation is by cuttings in summer.

FORSYTHIA Oleaceae

Eastern Asia. Forsythias are really shrubs for the open border in Britain but serve to cover a north or east wall and can prove to be very decorative and colourful.

F. suspensa This is particularly attractive in early spring but needs to be trained and the pruning of a young forsythia to cover a given wall space requires patience over several seasons. The pruning is to encourage strong, healthy stems or leaders for tying in and making a framework in whichever direction they are required to grow.

Mulch after flowering, and then prune the leading shoots back to about half their length to 2 or 3 selected buds which will then produce further strong shoots. These should be tied in at intervals during the year. The same process of pruning and tying in subsequent growth should be carried out until the whole allotted space has been filled. Lateral growths which have flowered should also be pruned back immediately after flowering to 5–7cm (2–2.5in) of that year's growth. This method of pruning is essential to keep the plant confined to the wall and free of untidy, straggly growth. It is deciduous and the flowers are golden yellow and open in April. Forsythias love abundant sunshine and a rich, loamy soil.

Forsythia x *intermedia* 'Beatrix Farrand' This plant is a tetraploid with exceedingly large yellow flowers up to 4cm (1.5in) across, which appear during March and April and are startlingly exquisite in shape and form. They are excellent for cutting for the house.

FREMONTODENDRON Sterculiaceae

F. Californicum A shrub or small tree, partially evergreen and is best with wall protection in the warmer areas of Britain. It will grow several metres high but will be cut down in a severe winter. The leaves are 5–9cm (2–3.5in) long, three-lobed and felted on the underside as are the stems which have rust coloured hairs. It is ideal for the sheltered sunny angle of two walls. The flowers appear in late summer and these are really large sepals 5–7cm (2–2.5in) across and are of a rich golden-yellow with a waxy texture. Purchase 'California Glory' which is larger and has greater vigour than either of its parents, *F. californicum* and *F. mexicanum*. This is a free-flowering form and should be widely available in nurseries and garden centres.

FUCHSIA Onagraceae

Although in no way can a Fuchsia be considered a climber, if planted at the foot of a wall it can be most attractive and will flower earlier and all the more readily. It will also be less likely to be cut to the ground in a severe winter.

F. magellanica gracilis 'Variegata' This plant has grey-green leaves flushed with pink and with a white edge. The flowers are fuchsia-red and purple.

F. m. 'Versicolor' The leaves are grey-green, variously rose tinted and variegated with creamy white.

F. molinae 'Sharpitor' The small green leaves have a cream edge and the very slender flowers are the palest of pinks. This was selected and propagated from a sport from the green at the National Trust property of that name within the last fifteen years.

F. m. 'Golden Fleece' This is the golden variegated clone to 'Sharpitor' with gold edged

Fig 31　Fuchsia magellanica gracilis *'Variegata'*.

leaves and the same slender pale pink flowers as 'Sharpitor'. This latter is possibly a very old clone, 'now re-discovered', and it seems to be popular with nurserymen at the moment.

F. m. **'Aurea'**　This is a clone with golden yellow leaves and flowers of a deep fuchsia red.

Cultural Notes　All the fuchsias mentioned are hardy in all but the worst of winters. Any good soil is suitable. Propagate from soft wood cuttings taken in late summer. Young plants should be overwintered in frost free conditions.

GARRYA Garryaceae (Tassel Bush)

G. elliptica　USA. This is an evergreen, bushy shrub and can be quite vigorous in growth once established. It can grow 2–4m (6.5–13ft) high when against a wall and has shiny, dark green leaves above, grey and woolly beneath. The real attraction of this shrub are the long, slender, hanging male catkins, 7–12cm (3–4in) long. These are formed of silvery clusters of flowers. This is an ideal plant for north and east facing walls. The flowers are borne in November at a time when there is little else of interest in the garden. Be sure to ask for and obtain a plant that is male for female catkins are nowhere near as large and long.

Cultural Notes　This shrub likes a light loamy soil with good drainage and full sun.

HEDERA Araliaceae (Ivy)

This subject is dealt with more fully in a separate section, *see* pages 94–105.

HIBISCUS Malvaceae

A deciduous shrub, *Hibiscus* benefits from wall treatment particularly in the north and the colder areas of Britain. It grows up to 3m (10ft) or more, the leaves are most attractive in that they are ovate, toothed or lobed and of a neutral green. The beauty of this shrub is that the flowers which appear from August onwards can be obtained in colours ranging from white, pink, through to deep, wine red, and blue. There are single and double forms.

Cultural Notes In the past, the general practice was not to prune this shrub other than the removal of dead wood and weak growing shoots. In order to keep the plant within its allotted space, it is, however, important to cut back the previous year's growth in early spring. I have discovered that the plant does not seem to suffer by this radical pruning. In fact, it gave me more flowers and a more compact, well furnished plant.

HOHERIA Malvaceae

H. lyallii New Zealand. Two species are of interest as a wall shrub. This one bears bright green leaves quite downy on both surfaces and in July has clusters of white flowers 2–4cm (0.7–1.5in) in diameter with a central boss of purple stamens. It is reasonably hardy.

H. sexstylosa This is evergreen, somewhat more erect in growth habit than the previous species and is similarly tolerably hardy in Great Britain when grown against a wall. It is a most attractive plant when in flower which are clusters of white 2cm (0.7in) flowers. There is a variegated form of this latter species which I have seen growing most successfully as a wall shrub in the Southampton area and in a park in the Isle of Wight.

Cultural Notes Suitable for most soils even those with a lime content.

HOLBOELLIA Lardizabalaceae

H. coriacea Asia. An evergreen, twining climber which is the hardier of the two species grown in this country. It is a vigorous climber of up to 6m (20ft) and has dark, glossy green, leathery leaves. The purplish female and the greenish-white male flowers are borne in separate clusters during April. Very occasionally, the flowers are followed by purple fruits which are sausage-shaped and contain jet black seeds.

H. latifolia This second species is less hardy but the flowers are exceedingly fragrant.

Cultural Notes Both species can be propagated by seed or cuttings of semi-ripe wood.

HUMULUS Cannabidaceae (Hop)

If you have the space, no garden should be without a hop. There are two species of these herbaceous, perennial twiners. The female flowers grow within the broad overlapping bracts which are cone-like. These provide the hops of commerce.

H. japonicus Coming from Asia, this climbs 6m (20ft) or more in a season and has leaves up to 12cm (5in) long and as wide. There is a wonderful dramatic form in *H. j.* 'Variegatus' in which the leaves are splashed and streaked with white. Whenever I have grown this, even in the mildest of winters, it has never proved to be truly perennial.

H. lupulus This is the common or European hop and is normally green. However, I recommend that you purchase *H. l.* 'Aureus', the leaves of which are a glorious golden yellow. It revels in sunlight and certainly brightens up a dull wall or similar structure. I have grown, for some twenty years or more, a form which I think of as variegated. It was found in a Kent hopfield and its leaves are a blotchy mixture of both green and gold. This has provided me with a talking point

Fig 32   Humulus lupulus *'Taff's Variegated'.*

Fig 33   Humulus lupulus *'Taffs Variegated' with young growth.*

amongst collectors of the unusual. For this reason, I have maintained its distribution within a narrow circle of enthusiasts. However, with the need for conservation, it has now been distributed from my garden to an ever widening group of people so that I hope that it will remain an oddity and collectors' item for many years.

Cultural Notes   Propagated by cuttings of basal shoots in spring.

HYDRANGEA *Hydrangeaceae*

H. petiolaris   Far East. This is the most widely grown of the climbing species of *Hydrangea*. It is deciduous with roundish, slightly ovate leaves which are slightly toothed. The flattish heads of the lace-like flowers are white and surrounding these heads are four-petalled white sterile larger flowers which are held on stalks. These flowers will age and fade to a dull brown. It is a vigorous climber by means of rootlets rather like those of ivy. It is ideal for a west or north wall. On the latter, it seems to be more floriferous but not as vigorous in growth.

Cultural Notes   Plant in rich, moist, leafy loam. Prune to keep within bounds. Propagate by layering or cuttings.

HYPERICUM *Guttiferae*

H. leschenaultii   Java. One does not normally associate *Hypericum* with climbers. However, this species makes an excellent, almost evergreen

Fig 34   Clematis texensis 'Gravetye Beauty' scrambling through Hydrangea macrophylla 'Tricolor', the lace-cap Hydrangea, said to be a branch sport of the cultivar 'Maresii'.

Fig 35   *Careful pruning of side shoots produces good results.*

wall shrub of lax habit. If the leading shoots are trained over wires attached to the wall and the lateral shoots allowed to hang down in a trailing manner, this plant can be most attractive. The flowers are a rich golden yellow, about 8cm (3in) across and are borne singly, in threes or in clusters of seven. The leaves are ovate to oblong. It blooms usually from July to the end of September. It can be given extra protection by planting it close behind or in between more hardy shrubs which will give it shelter. The colour of the flowers is such a rich, showy yellow that it is worth giving the shrub a trial against a warm sheltered wall. It must be admitted that this is only suitable for the mildest of localities but is excellent on the wall in a large conservatory.

Cultural Notes   Grows well in a loose loamy soil. Propagation is by cuttings.

IPOMOEA *Convolvulaceae*

Refer to the section on Annuals on pages 114–117.

ITEA *Escalloniaceae*

I. ilicifolia   Far East. This is an elegant shrub and is evergreen with holly-like foliage. The flowers are rather small, greenish-white florets that hang in profusion in catkin-like streamers and are sweetly scented. Flowering begins in August and in a mild autumn, continues for many weeks. This shrub is not totally hardy in Britain and thus is best grown against a wall for protection and it has the advantage that it will grow well on a north wall with soil that will not dry out.

JASMINUM *Oleaceae* (Jasmine)

There are many jasmines that are suitable for walls, however, none are truly climbers but because of their lax habit, they do need support of some kind.

J. nudiflorum (Winter Jasmine)   This provides us with cheering winter blooms of bright yellow 2cm (0.8in) or more wide and as long. Plantings of this shrub are usually a tangled mass through lack of pruning and attention. It is best clipped back after flowering to cut out the old flowered wood and any shoots that have died back in order to maintain plenty of young flowering stems. These should also be periodically tied in to fill the allotted space – in height this is usually no more than 3m (l0ft). The shoots should be tied in to the framework of the wall or trellis. Catalogues usually offer just the one form which bears pairs of trifoliate glossy green leaves on green stems for the first year, and older wood is chocolate brown.

There is a form *J. nudiflorum aureum* with leaves that are blotched yellow. This yellow blotching appears at its best with the commencement of spring and sunlight on the young growth causes the leaves to take on the lovely, blotched, golden colour. The overall effect is that of a golden mass of leaves, an added bonus and attraction. I believe that I was instrumental in re-introducing this form to the trade after having seen it after the war in a large, neglected and overgrown garden. Its flowers are the same size and quality as the green form. At the time, I did not know of its existence and was much taken with this find. It is fully hardy in most areas with growths capable of reaching 9m (29ft) in length. It blooms from midsummer through to October constantly throwing out clusters of small white trumpet flowers.

J. n. 'Variegata'   More recently, I was able to obtain from Japan, a white-edged variegated *Jasminum nudiflorum*. This plant has leaves that have a thin white edge. I have established that a plant of this description was recorded in the early 1900s in writings of collectors of the unusual. It was, apparently, rare and not generally available in commerce. It is a weak grower to only 2m (6.5ft), probably because of the lesser quantity of chlorophyll in its leaves. However, it seems to be just as hardy as the green form and will, I hope, be a plant eagerly sought out by enthusiasts. As yet, I do not think it is available in the trade in this country.

J. officinale   This is the summer flowering jasmine and has been grown in British gardens for so long that its date of introduction is not known. It bears masses of fragrant white flowers from July onwards. The plant makes a tangled mass of

Fig 36   Jasminum officinale *'Aureovariegatum'*.

Fig 37 Jasminum officinale 'Aureovariegatum' scrambling through a yew tree.

growth and is ideal for growing over garden structures such as an arbour and will readily cover the side of a summerhouse and can be tied in and trained against a lattice of wood or wire. The pinnate leaves are composed of 5–7 leaflets.

J. o. **'Aureovariegatum'** There are two coloured leaved forms, *Jasminum* 'Aureovariegatum' has bright, orange-yellow leaf variegation in a splashed, irregular pattern. This can be quite striking when grown over a dark green shrub or with a foil of dark green shrubs adjacent.

J. o. **'Argenteovariegatum'** This plant has a somewhat more restrained colouring to its leaves in that they are mainly edged with a creamy-white. However, in full sun, the young, new growth is quite creamy-yellow with a flush of pink edging to the extremities of the leaves. The

centre of the leaves are irregularly green and grey. Both the forms mentioned are now more readily available from the specialist nurserymen who are appreciating that many gardeners enjoy growing the unusual for pleasure. I have grown both these forms in two gardens over a span of thirty years with great success and have recently been distributing cutting material so that these plants will be enjoyed by those who would like to grow something out of the ordinary.

I recently found in a Dutch nursery a superb clone that has only golden leaves and this is proving to be quite dramatic when grown against green shrubs. The Dutch nursery in question did not feel that this golden form had any commercial possibilities, but we shall see. It will be available through some specialist nurseries.

J. x *stephanense* This is a hybrid between *J. beesianum* and *J. officinale*. The leaves are those of *officinale* but it has scented, light pink flowers followed by glossy black berries. The young leaves are mottled creamy-white.

J. beesianum This is a deciduous semi-twiner with leaves that are ovate to lanceolate, 3–5cm (1–1.5in) long and are of a deep green. The fragrant flowers are small, red to carmine in colour and 1.5cm (0.5in) long.

Cultural Notes These are completely hardy in Great Britain. Any good soil is suitable. Propagate with cuttings of half-ripened wood.

KADSURA *Schisandraceae*

K. japonica Far East. A twining evergreen, it will thrive outside in a sheltered site in Britain. Native to China, it can grow, if happy, to 2m (6.5ft) or more in height. The glossy green leaves are 5–10cm (1.5–4in) long and it flowers from late summer to autumn. The flowers are solitary, cream in colour, 2cm (0.8in) wide and composed of 6–9 rather fleshy textured petals. The fruits are red berries.

Fig 38   The more conventional gazebo will enhance a corner of the
larger garden and will provide a tranquil area for studying, taking tea or
just sitting. Gazebos have come down to us through the ages and were
important structures in famous gardens. They have been variously known
as pagodas, grottos, temples, tea houses, pavilions and summer houses in
their various forms, sizes and periods. By whatever name they are known
today, they act as a centre for personal retreat from the day-to-day
chores and the pressures of present-day living. There is no better way to
end a terrace or long pathway than with a gazebo.

Cultural Notes   Grows in any good garden soil. Propagate from summer cuttings.

K. j. 'Variegata'   This has cream-white bordered leaves. A less vigorous climber but worth growing for the unusual variegated leaves. This is seldom offered in commerce; seek out cutting material from an established plant.

LAPAGERIA Philesiaceae

Chile. A twining evergreen growing to 4–5m (13–16ft), with leathery textured leaves which are ovate and up to 10cm (4in) in length. The flowers are six-petalled, bell-shaped and of a waxy texture.

L. rosea   This has crimson flowers, the variety *L. albiflora* has white flowers. Flowering is from midsummer to autumn. It can be only grown out of doors in southern maritime counties against a shaded site. When in full bloom it presents a spectacle that is hard to beat. The form 'Nash Court', probably a hybrid, has soft pink flowers. For those who have conservatories, this plant can be grown well in a large tub providing that the conservatory is frost free. Out of doors, protection from winter wind and cold can be provided by a sheet of polythene of the 'bubble' type, tied at the two uppermost points at the top of the plant with the bottom of the sheet pegged into the ground and tucked in around the lower growths. It is well worth trying to grow this plant simply for the flowers.

LATHYRUS Leguminosae

A genus of both annuals and perennials including the familiar and well-known annual sweet pea and the scentless perennial everlasting pea. It is more usual to see tripods or rows of canes or pea sticks or some form of structure to grow the annual sweet pea of which there are many and diverse colour forms. Some are highly perfumed. They do not lend themselves to wall culture nor do they need it.

Fig 39   A wigwam of canes in a large pot or tub. Ideal for growing sweet peas.

Cultural Notes   Annuals and perennials alike can be raised from seed. Perennials can be divided or raised from basal cuttings. Grow in good rich soil.

L. latifolius   This is the everlasting pea and is a perennial, clump-forming plant sending up stems to 3–4m (10–13ft) or more annually. Although without scent, the flowers are quite attractive and can be very useful for cut flowers for the house. Whilst the usual colour of flower is rosy-purple, there is an excellent pure white form more usually known as 'White Pearl' although some authorities have listed it as 'Snow Queen'. Also quite attractive is a pink form, again sometimes called 'Pink Pearl' or 'Roseus'.

L. nervosus 'Lord Anson's Pea' A perennial of purplish blue and a touch of white in the small flowers and this is most attractive. It has been the subject of considerable agitation by the National Council for the Conservation of Plants and Gardens lest this be lost to cultivation. It can reach a height of lm (3.3ft) though often it is less. The flowers are produced in the leaf axils and remain close to the glaucous foliage. The flowering season lasts for several weeks. Whilst this is very dainty when in flower, it is undoubtedly a collector's item. Some authorities call this *Lathyrus magellanicus* and to make matters even more complicated, some seedsmen offer a small, blue flowered annual as 'Lord Anson's Pea'. This is more correctly named as *L. sativus*.

L. odoratus This is the original sweet pea, an annual with highly scented flowers. The species, *L. odoratus*, has purple flowers. However, today we can obtain the highly bred and selected sweet pea so that the choice of what to grow depends on the colours and heights preferred. It still can be fun to seek out from specialist seedsmen some of the early *L. odoratus* self-coloured forms which are so intensely perfumed. Of

Fig 40 Lathyrus latifolius *'White Pearl'.*

Fig 41 *'White Pearl' twining on a trellis.*

these, I particularly favour 'Painted Lady' which is a bi-colour of pink and white. Save the seed from year to year of these old forms.

L. rotundifolius   This is the Persian everlasting pea, climbing to a metre or so with flowers of a rose colour which are 2cm (0.8in) wide and there are usually 3–8 flowers in a raceme.

L. tuberosus   A perennial with creeping root-stock that has flowers early in the summer of a lovely, clear deep pink.

LONICERA Caprifoliaceae
(Honeysuckle)

This genus are valued chiefly for their fragrant flowers and some for their berries. All will do well in a good loamy soil that does not dry out. Nearly all the climbers and twiners in the genus are happy in semi-shade. They only need pruning to be kept in bounds and to thin out weak and straggly growth. To be at their best and to furnish the plant well, they need to be regularly tied in.

Cultural Notes   All honeysuckles can be pro-pagated from half ripened wood cuttings in July.

L. x americana (L. caprifolium x L. etrusca)
This hybrid is vigorous and free with its fragrant white flowers which age through cream to deep yellow with the outers flushed purple. Flowers are borne profusely when against a wall, from late April through to the main display in June–July. This is an ideal plant for walls, though excellent over small trees, pergolas or summerhouses.

L. x brownii   This is another cross, almost ever-green and only moderately vigorous. The flowers, 2.5–4cm (1–1.5in) long, are borne in whorls and are of a rich orange-scarlet. Perhaps the best clone to obtain is 'Dropmore Scarlet'. This is a hybrid with the more tender *L. sempervirens* hail-ing from the USA. The flowers of 'Dropmore Scarlet' very much resemble *L. sempervirens* and are more hardy than those of the species.

Fig 42   Four canes inserted into a tub or planter to train honeysuckle makes an excellent pyramid-shaped focal point for patio or terrace.

L. caprifolium   This is an early honeysuckle, possibly a British native, producing intensely fragrant cream flowers, the buds barely tinged with pink, in early summer.

L. x heckrottii   'Gold Flame' is a second gener-ation cross presumed to be *L. x americana* and *L. x sempervirens*. It is a scrambler and needs to be well tied in but is not too rampant a grower. Its

55

superior flowers commend it to space in the garden as it has pinnacle-like copious clusters of flowers which are yellow, red budded and fragrant.

L. henryi The 2cm (0.8in) long flowers are yellow, red-purple flushed in summer and are borne in terminal clusters. Its greatest attribute is possibly the gorgeous blue-black berries.

L. japonica A fast growing evergreen climber and possibly my favourite of this species is *L. j. aureoreticulata*. This has small broad leaves, sometimes lobed, with the veins markedly yellow giving a 'netted' effect. The flowers are white, flushed purple and are fragrant. I find that this honeysuckle, if left with 2–3 years growth, can get out of hand and become top heavy. I therefore recommend giving it a good hair cut, down to 1m (3.3ft), every other year, to enjoy the young, beautifully marked leaves.

Fig 43   Lonicera sempervirens.

Fig 44   Lonicera. *Late Dutch.*

Fig 45   Lonicera. *Early Dutch.*

L. periclymenum   This is our common honey-suckle or woodbine. The flowers are a creamy-white and age to yellow. Some plants have the buds flushed purple and these are usually known in the trade as early Dutch honeysuckle. The late Dutch honeysuckle, flowering from July onwards has flowers which are soft purple-pinkish within.

L. x tellmanniana   This is a plant for shade. The 5cm (2in) flowers of a rich coppery-yellow are borne in June and July but are not fragrant. It is deciduous and climbs to 6m (20ft).

L. tragophylla   This honeysuckle is one of the parents of the above and is even more spec-tacular. It again needs a shady site to do well and to provide the lovely terminal clusters of very large butter-yellow 6–9cm (2.5–3.5in) flowers. Although not scented, these are an absolute eye-catcher.

MUEHLENBECKIA *Polygonaceae*

M. complexa   New Zealand. Whilst this is classified as deciduous and not entirely hardy everywhere in Britain it is ideal for covering an old tree stump or an uninteresting structure. Its leaves are borne on black-purple wiry stems and most of the leaves are perfect replicas of a fiddle. For this feature alone, it is certainly a curiosity. The flowers that are greenish-white are in-significant.

Cultural Notes   Can be propagated by cuttings taken in summer.

MUTISIA *Compositae*

South America. This is a genus of climbing plants in the daisy family and possessing leaf tipped tendrils. Although neither of the two species mentioned here are entirely hardy, they are perhaps worth cossetting and once planted, should not be disturbed.

Cultural Notes Propagate from cuttings or seed. As both these plants sucker, the failure of both plant and suckers will ensue if any effort is made to dig them up.

M. ilicifolia This has holly-like, leathery leaves of 6cm (2.5in) long. The 6cm (2.5in) flowers are pink to mauve and open from spring to late summer.

M. oligodon It is only a partial climber and prefers acting like a trailer. It has 3cm (1in) oblong, leathery spiny-toothed leaves that are glossy green above and have a whitish woolly texture beneath. The flowers are daisy-like and are a clear pink.

MYRTUS Myrtaceae (Myrtle)

A neat and beautiful shrub, the leaves, when rubbed in the hand, give a satisfying aroma.

M. communis The common myrtle grows well in all but the colder counties of Britain. It will do best tucked in against a south wall. If it is content it will grow to 9m (30ft) and will be covered in lustrous, dark green leaves. The flowers, appearing in July, are small, white and have a dense, fluffy brush of stamens protruding from the petals and are sweetly scented. The fruits are a dusky purple.

M. communis 'Variegata' This has leaves edged with cream to yellow.

M. communis tarentina This is more compact with smaller leaves. There is also a variegated form which has white edged leaves. There are other myrtles such as *M. luma* and *M. ugni*, also with their variegated counterparts but these, unfortunately, are only suitable for the

milder counties in the south-west and even then will need wall protection.

OLEARIA Compositae
(Daisy Bush)

O. erubescens Although really half-hardy, hailing from Australia, it really is worth finding a niche for this against a wall and in sun. It is an excellent plant for covering the base of wall climbers such as clematis and honeysuckle. The alternate leaves are stiff and leathery, oval to oblong with coarse, marginal teeth. They are 2–4cm (0.8in–1.5in) long, and shiny green with the underneath having a brown heavy texture. The flowers produced on the previous year's growth have a yellow central disk with 3–5 ray-florets.

Cultural Notes Propagate by cuttings taken in late summer.

O. erubescens var. *ilicifolia* Look for the variety 'ilicifolia'. This has larger flower heads and somewhat larger leaves. It prefers a light, well drained soil.

OSMANTHUS Oleaceae

O. delavayi China. This makes an excellent evergreen wall plant and seems to be quite happy on a north wall. It is fairly slow growing and does well on chalk soil. The glossy, dark green, oval to ovate toothed leaves are 1.5–2.5cm (0.5–1in) long. The white flowers are deliciously scented and are borne in small clusters. The berries are somewhat oblong and bluish-black in colour when ripe. Its slender, stiffish shoots are wreathed in April from nearly end to end with the white flowers. This is a spectacular sight.

Coming to us from the Far East, including Japan are shrubs that are quite capable of being free standing, but in hard winters can be severely cut back by cold frosts. Therefore, to enjoy their beautifully crafted, holly-like leaves, I recommend that you grow them close to a warm wall for the added protection that this will give. However, if planted 0.5m (2ft) distant from the wall and in reasonable shelter from wind, you can still put a climbing plant behind them. They can be kept pruned back to 1m (3.3ft) or so high and, with the attraction of their leaves, make a superb focal point.

Cultural Notes Pruning should be done to keep the plant within bounds and this should be carried out immediately after flowering. Propagate with half ripe wood cuttings taken in summer.

O. heterophyllus 'Aureus' With rich gold leaves.

O. h. 'Aureomarginatus' Leaves are margined with deep golden yellow.

O. h. 'Argenteomarginatus' With white margined leaves.

O. h. 'Purpureus' Leaves of a quite dark purple.

O. h. tricolor (Goshiki) Green leaves splashed with white, suffused pink.

PAEONIA *Paeoniaceae* (Tree Peony)

China. A really hardy plant and quite suitable for a north wall. If too warm a wall, the precocious growth of flower buds can be killed by late spring frosts. They like a deep rich soil which should be manured before planting. They grow equally well on acid or limey soils. There are many clones available from the nurseryman. As well as single flowered forms, there are superb double forms, all in a wide range of colours. These are plants that need space and the strong growths need to be tied in to either a series of stakes or training wires affixed to a wall or fence.

Cultural Notes Propagation is usually by seed.

PARTHENOCISSUS *Vitaceae*

Generally referred to as Virginia Creeper, albeit incorrectly.

P. henryana This has superb velvety leaves with a bronze flush, consisting of 3–5 leaflets. These leaves are marked with silvery-white and pink

Fig 46 A lightweight wall trellis – ideal for a clematis or Tropaeolum but not for climbers with a heavy weight of plant material.

Fig 47   Set the scene with an archway and trellis clothed with climbing plants, preparing the eyes of one's friends for the delights of this garden that you have created. Keep the plants well trained in, twisting the new growths around the uprights and along the top. This makes a handsome backdrop for foreground planting.

along the veins, particularly on the young leaves. The best colour of the young growths is shown when grown on a north or north-west wall and in partial shade. The leaves turn a deep crimson in the autumn. This is a self-clinging climber, deciduous and with vigorous growth. Small, dark blue grapes are sometimes produced.

Cultural Notes   Cut back in late autumn after leaf fall to keep it within bounds. It does not resent hard pruning during the growing season if it is around windows, doors, etc.

P. quinquefolia   This is the true Virginia Creeper hailing from the USA. A vigorous climber, it can reach to over 15m (50ft) when happy and it is a self-clinger. The leaves are usually 5-lobed which turn to a glorious flame red in autumn.

P. tricuspidata   This is the 'Boston Ivy' often wrongly called Virginia Creeper and it comes from Japan. The leaves are variously 3- or 5-lobed, toothed, and a bright green turning to rich crimson and orange in autumn. It is an excellent and deciduous wall climber on north or east walls. Because of its vigour, it is not one for a bungalow or a dwarf wall. Should you be unfortunate enough to have an unsightly structure in your garden, this is an ideal climber with which to clothe it. The waxy-looking blue fruits are rather hidden by the mass of leaves. Should you have reason to cut down a Parthenocissus, marks will be left on your brick or stonework to which the pads have adhered, but the use of a wire brush will quickly remove these.

Cultural Notes   Prune back as required, most likely in mid-summer, if it proves to be too invasive.

PASSIFLORA *Passifloraceae*
(Passion Flower)

There are several species of *Passiflora* and many can be used as annuals if started from seed or cuttings.

P. antioquiensis   This, in particular, has very showy rose red flowers with purple stamens. It makes an excellent climber for a frost-free greenhouse or conservatory. I recommend this

plant to you for the beauty and colour of its flowers.

P. caerulea   No less showy than the above and surprisingly hardy in Britain although it can be cut back to ground level in a cold winter. It will usually spring up again and is capable of growing 10m (33ft) in a season, climbing by tendrils. The leaves are deeply 5–9 lobed and dark green. It is best on a south facing sheltered wall. In the colder parts of the country, it is best perhaps in an unheated greenhouse or conservatory. The structure of the flowers are said to be the symbols of the instruments of Christ's passion. The three stigmas represent the three nails, the five stamens, the five wounds, the ring of filaments within the sepals, the crown of thorns and the ten sepals represent the ten apostles. The tendrils and hand-like leaves represent the hands

Fig 48   The flower of Passiflora caerulea.

Fig 49 A successful grouping of pots and climbing plants.

and whips of Christ's persecutors. The showy, five-petalled blue flowers backed by light green sepals are flat when open in the sun. They bloom from July until the autumn frosts. The large, ovoid, orange coloured fruits are sometimes produced during long hot summers. There is a cultivar 'Constance Elliott' with ivory white flowers but in all other respects is the same as the other species. Due to the vigorous growth, this plant needs tying to training wires or the like for, in gusty weather, I have known the sheer weight of top growth to pull away from the wall, the tendrils not always being sufficiently strong to anchor it safely.

Cultural Notes   Easily propagated by seed or cuttings and requires a good, deep soil.

PENSTEMON Scrophulariaceae

P. cordifolius   Whilst the penstemons of the herbaceous border or the rock garden are familiar to most gardeners, it is unfortunate that this glorious shrubby plant is so little known.

Its toothed and pointed leaves are heart-shaped and 2–3cm (0.8–1in) long. The exquisite scarlet flowers are tubular of typical penstemon form and these bloom from midsummer till autumn. The shoots need tying back to the wall as its growth is rather lax and floppy. It is ideal to plant beneath a window on a warm wall in a mild district. It is a great pity that this plant is not more widely grown and even more surprising that there are only two nurseries in the Plant Finder that offer it.

Cultural Notes   Prune moderately hard before growth commences in April. It prefers a well-drained soil.

PERIPLOCA Asclepiadaceae
(Silk Vine)

P. graeca   The more readily obtainable Silk Vine and the most hardy. It is a deciduous twiner of over 6m (20ft) and has shiny, dark green oval leaves. The flowers are brownish purple with buds of greenish yellow. These are borne in clusters in summer and have a heavy peculiar smell. The seed pods are in pairs, 8cm (3in) or more long and joined at the tips. The seeds within the pods bear 3cm (1in) long tufts of silky hairs, hence the common name of the Silk Vine. This is an ideal plant for growing over dead trees or an unsightly building and grows rapidly. The plant would be quite suitable for an arbour or grown up a pole that needs softening with Nature's growth. It is a plant of interest rather than beauty.

Cultural Notes   Grows well in any ordinary garden soil. Take cuttings in summer or sow seed.

PEROVSKIA Labiatae

P. atriplicifolia   From a perennial root stock, semi-woody stems are produced with grey-green leaves which in August to September have panicles of small, violet-blue flowers. Seek out the cultivar 'Blue Spire' for this is undoubtedly the best form. In a cold winter, growths can be cut back and should have such dead wood cut out in the spring. An ideal plant for a wall beneath a window or used as a screen to hide the bare stems of other wall climbers.

PHILADELPHUS Hydrangeaceae
(erroneously known as Syringa)

The only reason for growing this on a wall, which should be near an open window, is to enjoy the rich perfume of its blossoms. Some of the species and cultivars are quite tall growing and would normally be grown as free standing shrubs in the garden. It is essential wherever they are grown that you should thin out and cut back immediately after flowering. Cut down the old flowering shoots to within a few cms of the old wood. If grown on a wall, the treatment is exactly the same except that the current season's growth should be tied in to cover the allotted

63

space. Nearly all the cultivars have white flowers except for a few that have a pink to purple blotch deep inside the flowers.

P. 'Virginal'   My selection for a wall site is *P.* 'Virginal' which has double white flowers of 2–3cm (0.8–1in) across and are richly fragrant. It is undoubtedly the best of the double flowered cultivars.

P. coronarius 'Aureus'   This has superbly coloured golden leaves and is ideal for a dappled shade wall site to give a glow of brightness. It is quite suitable for dry soils.

P. c. 'Variegatus'   This has leaves widely edged with a creamy-white margin which can be quite dramatic in half shade. The shrub's leaves have a luminescence in this subdued light. This plant is often erroneously called 'Bowles' Form'.

P. 'Innocence'   This has leaves splashed with yellow and thrives happily in bright sunlight.

PHLOMIS Labiatae
(Jerusalem Sage)

This evergreen shrub grows best close to, if not actually against, a wall as its hardiness is suspect in the northern climes of Britain.

P. fruticosa   It can be useful to screen the bare lower stems of a wall climber and forms a large bush with its dull, grey-green, wrinkled and woolly leaves of 7–12cm (2.7–5in) long. The flowers are bright yellow 2–4cm (0.8–1.5in) long, borne in tight whorled clusters at the end of the shoots. Successfully grown, this is an ideal bush to act as a foil to train a clematis to scramble over and through it. The leaf texture and flowers give a warm Mediterranean feeling to the part of the garden in which it is grown.

Cultural Notes   This plant needs a hot, dry, sunny position. Propagate with young side shoots.

PHYGELIUS Scrophulariaceae
(Cape Figwort)

This is an excellent plant for south and west walls and should be planted in a well drained soil.

P. capensis   This has been grown for many years and was introduced from South Africa, hence its common name of Cape Figwort. It has often been grown against a wall of a walled garden in large estates. In most parts of the country, all growth above ground is cut down in winter. As the ground warms up, growths emanate from the woody rootstock below ground and rise to 1–2m (3.3–6.5ft) in a lax manner. These growths are clothed in lanceolate leaves terminating in panicles of red, tubular flowers which have a yellow throat. There is a count today of at least ten clones being offered with flowers ranging in colour from white to pink and very dark reds.

P. aequalis   This species is possibly a little more tender than the above. It has a similar range of named clones with flowers of white, yellow, cream or pink. These flowers are somewhat more pendulous than those of the above. The stout shoots may need staking or tying in.

PILEOSTEGIA Hydrangeaceae

P. viburnoides   Asia. A frost-hardy evergreen climber that is quite happy on a north facing or west wall, it is self-clinging and will run up to 10m (33ft) at least and needs space to show it at its best. The pairs of narrow oval leaves are 6–10cm (2.4–4in) long, are deep green and make an excellent foil for the panicles of tiny, creamy-white flowers that appear in autumn.

Cultural Notes   This plant needs a rich, moist soil. Propagate by cuttings in late summer or by layering in the spring.

Fig 50   Right: A simple arbour, clothed with a climbing hop, creating a dark background to complement an urn with silver planting.

PLUMBAGO *Plumbaginaceae*

P. capensis South Africa. An evergreen, slender stemmed scrambler, growing to 4m (13ft) but needs tying to its support. Because it is somewhat tender, it needs a wall site and during the summer, its branching stems terminate in 3–4cm (1.5–2in) long, sky blue flowers. For those of you that have the space but do not live in a mild district, this is an ideal plant for a conservatory or greenhouse and well worth growing for its long flowering season and its very pretty primrose-like flowers.

Cultural Notes Propagation is by summer cuttings.

POLYGONUM *Polygonaceae*
(Knotweed or Russian Vine)

There are many species in this genus but very few are climbers. Even fewer are worthy of space in the garden. However, they are often planted to cover an unwanted shed or other structure that is unsightly.

P. baldschuanicum This species has been nicknamed the 'Mile a Minute' plant. It has 5–10cm (2–4in) long leaves and panicles of tiny white bell-shaped flowers that can be tinged with pink and which appear in late summer and autumn. Indeed, it does grow very fast, but to my mind, there are many other more rewarding climbers.

PUERARIA *Leguminosae*
(Kudzu Vine)

Refer to section on Annual Climbers on pages 114–117.

PUNICA *Punicaceae*
(Pomegranate)

P. granatum Although this plant is not really hardy in Britain I have seen it growing against a wall in southern England.

P. g. 'Flore-pleno' There are several forms and perhaps the finest and the most ornamental being P. 'Flore-pleno'. It is a deciduous shrub with fresh green shiny leaves 5–7cm (2–3in) long and from July to September bears funnel-shaped orange-red flowers. There are records of plants existing in the countries bordering the Mediterranean, of the white flowered form.

P. granatum 'Nana' The usual form grown in this country is P. g. 'Nana', growing only 1–1.5m (3.3–5ft) high and when in flower it can be very decorative. This would be ideal for a patio garden against a wall. Fruit is seldom set in this country.

PYRACANTHA *Rosaceae*
(Fire Thorn)

While most pyracanthas are hardy and can be free standing, they make a wonderful wall-hugging shrub. Their growths can be trained to mould them around corners and curves and to lead them along walls and around windows. This should be done by using training wires or suitable trellis but take care as they are thorny. The evergreen foliage is dark, glossy green and these leaves are densely packed together. Pyracanthas can be bonus plants as they bear masses of white to pink flowers in June which are followed in due course by the main attraction, the berries. These plants prefer warmer walls in the north of England in order to ripen the wood and to produce a good crop of berries. In some districts, these berries are a great attraction and last for a long time. However, they are also attractive to birds and in no time at all, should the birds take a liking to them, the shrub can be stripped in a few days.

P. coccinea 'Lalandei' This is the most popular pyracantha for a wall and is at its best with berries in September. There are recently raised cultivars which have, in addition to their larger, brighter berries, a resistance to a fungal trouble known as scab. This causes spoiling of the berries, leaf drop and die back.

Fig 5I   Pyracantha 'Mohave', well trained for fourteen years in espalier
fashion. It has rich orange berries.

Fig 52   *Close up of the berries of Pyracantha.*

Fig 53   Pyracantha *coccinea with darker red berries.*

Fig 54   Cotoneaster *'Hybridus Pendulus' red berries on a weeping tree.*

P. x 'Mohave'   Among the best of the hybrids is 'Mohave' with large, orange-red berries.

P. x 'Telstar'   This has somewhat smaller dark crimson berries.

P. rogersiana   One of the parents of the previously mentioned hybrids. A less robust grower and has orange berries. This has a fine, bright yellow berried variety 'Flava'. This is most attractive and for reasons best known to the birds, is either avoided or left until there is no other berry food available. Such berries can stay, unattacked, until well into the New Year.

For those of you who would wish to grow pyracantha along a bare wooden fence, a shed wall or any similar vertical structure, there is a practice of training to be commended. This is to train it as an espalier form by running up a main shoot and allowing lateral branches to grow out from it every 30cm (1ft) or so, training them horizontally. Rub out all unwanted buds or incipient young shoots, particularly those growing inwards to the wall. It can be led around porches, in fact, this is a plant that you can lead almost anywhere. I have seen the results of a fifteen-year training of four pyracantha plants grown in this espalier manner, along a low fence, facing south and forming a barrier between two properties. It has been a great pleasure and provides considerable satisfaction to the grower. I hope that you will accept this challenge and try to grow pyracantha in this way.

PYROSTEGIA *Bignoniaceae*

P. venusta   Brazil. This is a spectacular tendril climber. It will trail along the ground or it can be trained to climb a high wall. It has rich, golden-orange flowers that appear on the leaf axils in late winter and spring. This is a frost tender plant and really only suitable for the milder southern counties of England. You will be well rewarded by its show of flowers if you can give it the conditions that it likes, that is *good* fertile soil and a sunny spot.

Cultural Notes   Raise from summer cuttings.

RHODOCHITON *Scrophulariaceae*

Refer to the section on Annuals on pages 114–117.

RHAMNUS *Rhamnaceae*

R. alaternus   This is an evergreen, bushy, rounded shrub usually growing to 3m (10ft). The shiny green leaves are 1cm (0.4in) or so long, somewhat oblong and abruptly pointed.

R. a. 'Variegata'   The leaves are pleasantly bordered with a creamy white and are somewhat narrower than the type.

Cultural Notes   As this plant suffers badly from wind buffeting, it needs the shelter of a wall particularly in its early years of growth. From my experience, the variegated form is not as hardy.

ROBINIA *Leguminosae*

R. hispida   This shrub is quite capable of being free standing and is hardy in Britain. Because its branches are so brittle and can be so easily broken by strong winds, it is often grown against a wall for the shelter that this gives. Its stems should be securely tied in to wires or wall ties. Any growths that face outwards and are awkward to tie back should be pruned back in late summer. The pink, pea-shaped flowers appear in June.

ROMNEYA *Papaveraceae*
(Tree Poppy)

R. coulteri   California. Once established, this is a beautiful plant which will reward you by flowering over a long season. It is a semi-shrubby perennial with blue-grey foliage. The flowers are large, white and poppy-like with large bunches of golden stamens. Flowering is from June till early autumn. This plant will take time to become established and resents any attempt to transplant it.

Cultural Notes   Treat this plant as an herbaceous perennial by cutting back the woody shoots to a few cms above ground each spring.

RUBUS *Rosaceae*

This genus has many prickly climbers or scramblers and quite deservedly warrant a place in any garden for their interesting and decorative foliage.

R. cissoides var. *pauperatus* (You might find this plant listed as *R. squarrosus* or *R. australis.*)   As an oddity, *R. c. pauperatus* has zig-zagging growths that are almost completely denuded of leaves and are armed with tiny white prickles. The flowers are yellowish-white and the plant will require wall shelter in most parts of Britain. In Australia and New Zealand, its nickname is the 'Barbed Wire Bramble' which is very apt.

R. laciniatus The fern-leaved bramble with very beautiful finely-cut leaves and is a form of our common blackberry. Like the blackberry, it is heavily armed. The fruits are large and juicy and the flavour is excellent.

If the cut-leaved attraction is a must, then look for the thornless blackberry. This is a very good plant if trained on a wall or pergola. However, the leaves are not quite so ferny-looking as the former.

R. cockburnianus There are several *Rubus* with a 'whitewashed' effect on the stems. This species is the best of them for on a cold, grey winter day, the stems look startlingly white and almost artificial.

Cultural Notes This species should be planted in a deep, rich loam which causes the stems to

grow more thick and white. Old wood and weak growths should be cut out in spring. Propagation is best carried out by tip layering of growths.

R. deliciosus Confine this to the wilder part of the garden, perhaps on a chain link fence, tying in the growths to enable you to enjoy the lovely white flowers which resemble a wild rose. The stems are thornless.

R. ulmifolius **'Bellidiflorus'** This has completely double flowers which are pink and these are borne profusely in panicles from July till autumn. This again is a plant for the wild garden and grows well in shade.

R. fruticosus **'Variegatus'** In this plant, the leaves are edged with quite a wide margin of creamy-white. When scrambling over a large shrub or trained to a wall, it is certainly eye-catching and constitutes a 'talking point' in any

Fig 55 Rubus fruticosus *'Variegatus'. A variegated blackberry with good edible fruits.*

Fig 56   Rubus phoenicolasius. *The Japanese wineberry. An excellent screen climber worth growing for its fruit and ornament.*

garden. It is a particularly good plant to grow up a stout post or trained where its handsome foliage can be best appreciated. This is the variegated form of the common wild blackberry and while the fruits are not variegated, they are edible and they look quite startling against the variegated leaves.

Cultural Notes   Grows in any good soil. Propagate by tip layering and prune out old wood and weak and dead shoots in the spring to promote new growth.

R. phoenicolasius   This is the Japanese wineberry. It makes an excellent screen climber and is well worth growing for its fruit and ornament. Its stems of 3m (10ft) are thickly set with red bristles and its trifoliate leaves of 10cm (4in) or more are broad and white felted beneath. The conical red fruits about 2cm (0.8in) long are sweet and juicy.

SCHISANDRA *Schisandraceae*

S. chinensis   The most hardy of the species. It is vigorous and has 1–2cm (0.4–0.8in) wide white to pink fragrant flowers in late spring. It bears spike-like fruiting clusters, the red fruits very much resembling a blackberry or raspberry. A male and female plant are needed to produce fruits.

S. rubriflora   A stemmed twiner with simple alternate leaves and unisexual flowers. One to several flowers are borne in the leaf axils. The fragrant flowers are deep crimson and the red, fruiting clusters are 6–10cm (2.5–4in) long. However, to enjoy the fruits, one needs to have both a male and a female plant growing close together. It needs plenty of room as it can grow to 10m (33ft) or so.

Cultural Notes   Grows in ordinary humus rich soil and is suitable for a wall in partial shade. Propagate by cuttings in late summer.

71

SCHIZOPHRAGMA
Hydrangeaceae

Members of this genus look very much like a climbing hydrangea and although closely related, they differ markedly to the botanist.

S. hydrangeoides Most commonly grown in cultivation is *S. hydrangeoides*. This is a deciduous climber with roundish, coarsely toothed leaves. The flower bracts are cream and there is a form with red bracts. These bloom in July and the plant can attain a height of 15m (50ft). This plant can look most attractive when it is in full bloom and climbing up a tree.

Cultural Notes Propagate by late summer cuttings.

SENECIO Compositae

S. macroglossus South Africa. This is not totally hardy but should grow well against a wall in dappled shade. Its nickname, Cape Ivy or Wax Vine are taken from the shape and texture of its glossy, dark green leaves. It can be often seen in its variegated form as a house plant in florists' shops and the greenhouses of garden centres with its ivy-like leaves that are edged in creamy-white. It has 5cm (2in) yellow flowers borne singly or in small terminal clusters. Cuttings of this plant have often been sent to me to be identified and I am asked 'what ivy is it'? This is because the leaves so characteristically resemble typical five-pointed ivy leaves.

S. mikanioides This is perhaps the hardiest in England of this climbing ragwort. It survives outside in the warmest areas and during the mildest of winters. It can attain growth to at least 6m (20ft) and has ivy-like glossy, green leaves. I have seen this plant climbing profusely and clothing rocky banks along sheltered walks in Jersey. The first time that I saw it, I thought it was an ivy because of its climbing ability, the similarity of its leaf outline and the way in which it clung.

Cultural Notes Both species are readily propagated by summer cuttings.

SMILAX Smilacaceae

This is a large genus of prickly stemmed tendril climbers, apt to form tangled, wiry thickets. Most are not really hardy and were very popular with Victorians who grew them for the architectural quality of their foliage and the usually, shiny green leaves. These were grown in pots or against a wall in their conservatories.

S. aspera Its superbly glossy, broadly ovate to narrow triangular leaves are 4–10cm (1.5–4in) in length. The smallish flowers are green and fragrant and open in summer. Red, glossy berries follow later in the year. I have grown the form, out of doors against a warm wall for many years and in two gardens, that has leaves blotched with white. This I have presumed to be, according to older reference works, *S. a.* var. *maculata*. I have always been well pleased with this plant and somewhat surprised by its hardiness for all references speak of its tenderness.

SOLANUM Solanaceae

S. capsicastrum This, in its green form, is very similar to that which is sold at Christmas-time but is more correctly named *S. pseudocapsicum* for its fruits are orange-red or scarlet. However, the variegated form of *S. capsicastrum* is most desirable and is more usually grown as a greenhouse sub shrub and grows to 1.5m–2m (5–6.5ft) high. If you are gardening in the south of England, try it against a sheltered wall, giving it a little winter protection with some litter around its roots or a polythene sheet hung over it and pegged down into the ground around it. The leaves, in this form, are edged with a good band of creamy-white. However, to me, the greatest attraction is the round 1.5cm (0.6in) berries which, in their early green state, are splashed with white variegation. These berries eventually turn to a bright orange-red, the variegation being

Fig 57   Solanum jasminoides

suffused and ultimately lost with the increased colouration.

Cultural Notes   Grows in any good garden soil and in the angle of two adjoining walls. Propagate with cuttings of half ripened wood in mid-summer.

S. crispum   This is a vigorous, semi-evergreen, lime tolerant sub shrub whose stems can rise to 4m (13ft) or more in a season. In June and July, it bears super purply-blue flowers which much resemble those of the normal garden potato. The form 'Glasnevin' is possibly hardier, its flowers continue from July into September.

S. dulcamara (Bittersweet/Woody Nightshade) A trailing or scrambling perennial that needs tying in. The leaves are ovate or cordate 2–4cm (0.8–1.5in) and slender pointed. The flowers are several drooping cymes, usually purple, in late summer and the fruit is red. I grow the variegated form with the leaves edged with a strong band of creamy-white. It always attracts attention, particularly if tied in fairly regularly so that the allotted space is well furnished.

SOPHORA *Leguminosae*

S. tetraptera   New Zealand. The leaves of this plant are alternate with leaflets opposite and very numerous. The flowers are panicle-like, pendulous racemes of beautiful, pea-like golden yellow and are borne during May and early June. The leaf and flower stalks have a browny down. This plant needs wall protection. The amusing long seed pods resemble necklaces in that they are somewhat bead-like in general appearance.

73

This is not a plant for small gardens for it can reach to a great height, is most difficult to train and cannot be expected to lie flat against a wall.

S. microphylla A smaller plant than the above and much more suitable therefore for the average house and garden. It too, has clusters of golden, tubular flowers in May and has the advantage of flowering at an earlier age.

TRACHELOSPERMUM
Apocynaceae (Star Jasmine)

T. asiaticum These are evergreen climbers, mainly coming from China and Japan. Two species interest us here. The first is *T. asiaticum*. This can densely clothe a wall and in a very satisfying way with its 2–5cm (0.8–2in) glossy, dark green leaves. It bears 2cm (0.8in) wide white flowers, ageing to yellow in late summer.

T. jasminoides This is possibly less hardy than *T. asiaticum* and is more of a twiner than a climber and thus needs the support of wires or trellis. The white flowers and the leaves are larger.

T. j. 'Variegatum' The leaves are irregularly margined with creamy-white edges.

T. j. 'Wilsonii' The leaves are rather more narrow but in the autumn these turn to a rich red colour.

T. j. 'Tricolor' A new introduction, this has leaves that are variously splashed with cream and suffused with blotches of red.

TRIPTERYGIUM Celastraceae

T. regelii Japan. A deciduous scrambling shrub that is hard to find today, even in special nurseries. It needs a lot of room and is perhaps best climbing into trees. It has handsome foliage, the leaves are 5–15cm (2–6in) long and are ovate to elliptical. In late summer, it bears large sprays of little greeny-white flowers followed by three-winged pale green fruits.

TROPAEOLUM Tropaeolaceae

Under this heading there are several perennial climbers which make annual growth and which die back to underground tubers. Annual *Tropaeolum* – the nasturtium – see the section on Annual Climbers on pages 114–117.

T. speciosum This is totally hardy. Its scarlet-crimson nasturtium-like flowers in late summer are most attractive when seen scrambling through evergreens. It bears bright blue fruits. It has a nickname, the Scottish flame flower, and can be seen at its best in the moist summers in Scotland which suit it admirably. This, perhaps, gives us a clue to its successful cultivation further south. This plant prefers a lime-free soil and some say that it prefers to have its roots intermingled with that of a hedge or shrub in moist soil. Excellent for a north wall and will climb on wires or trellis by its twining leaf stalks but sometimes needs assistance. The frail stems die down each year to fleshy roots. This is a plant that, if it likes you, will do well. If, after you have tried it in two or three places, you are not successful, try a different plant from another genus.

T. tuberosum There are other tuberous rooted tropaeolums and all are, unfortunately, somewhat tender. *T. tuberosum*, with broad, rounded, lobed leaves has large, orange and yellow tubular flowers. This is a must. Seek out the 'Ken Aslet' form. He was the former rock gardens' superintendent at the RHS gardens at Wisley. In this form, the flowers are elegantly borne on long, red stalks in early summer, whereas the previous available form under the name *T. tuberosum* used to flower in late summer and was consequently often killed by autumn frosts before it had flowered well.

Cultural Notes The specific name *tuberosum* refers to the potato-like tubers which are pear-

Fig 58 Tropaeolum tuberosum 'Ken Aslet'.

shaped, pale yellow with crimson splashed swellings. Each season, they multiply and pile up in the ground, one above the other. It is best that these tubers are removed from the ground in cold districts and stored in a box of damp peat in a frost-free garage or shed to await planting the following year as soon as the danger of frost has passed. Be careful not to let the box of peat dry out completely during the winter months.

VERONICA Scrophulariaceae

V. hulkeana New Zealand. A connoisseur's plant of outstanding beauty but none too hardy. It is certainly worth trying it on a sunny wall in a sheltered garden. It has a loose, straggly growth habit and therefore should have its leading shoots tied in to training wires and lateral shoots trained horizontally.

The evergreen leaves are coarsely toothed, oval, quite thick and of a lustrous, rich green. The erect flower panicles are 15cm (6in) long and half as wide and are of a lovely, delicate lavender

Fig 59 Tropaeolum tuberosum 'Ken Aslet' showing the bright, tubular flowers.

colour. These flowers are borne in great profusion so much so that the plant seems to be weighed down and burdened by its display. Flowering period is May to June. In order to assist this plant from being short-lived it is essential to remove all flowers that have faded and are going over. This action conserves the plant's energy and helps to keep it strong for it does have a tendency to exhaust itself to the point of death.

Cultural Notes   As an insurance, propagate by taking 15cm (6in) cuttings of young wood. This should be done every year in case your plant should fail. The surplus plants can always be given away should your plant maintain its vigour the following year.

VITIS Vitaceae

The ornamental species listed here have mainly large, rounded, often lobed leaves with greenish or yellow flowers. The fruits are bunches of grapes though, in these species, they are not edible. These plants are best suited as climbers over or up trees or on very large structures.

V. amurensis   A vigorous, hardy species, the leaves colour well in autumn, turning to crimson and purple.

V. coignetiae   A widely planted, superb vine for places where there is room for it to climb. It has leaves 10–20cm (4–8in) wide and sometimes

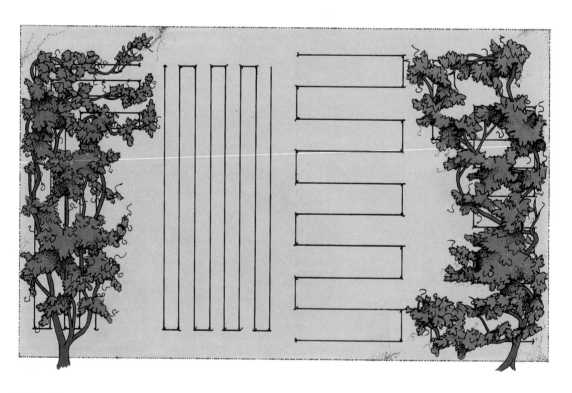

Fig 60   Alternative patterns, created with the aid of vine eyes, screw eyes and plastic covered wire, so arranged as to form a pattern upon which to train your climbers. These ideas are useful if you have the area to cover and wish for an alternative to the more regular pattern of crossed wires.

Fig 61 Stout wooden rough sawn timber makes an excellent pergola and when constructed over a pathway, is an ideal structure for Wisteria *or* Laburnum.

larger. These are a dark, russet brown underneath and colour to brilliant crimson to scarlet in autumn.

V. vinifera   This is a deciduous species growing to 10m (33ft) or more with deeply lobed, toothed, rounded leaves to 15cm (6in) wide. Often the undersides of the leaves are hairy. The green to amber or purple fruits are juicy and very variable in flavour.

***V. v.* 'Apiifolia'**   This is one of the more decorative forms and has deeply dissected foliage and hence its common name, the 'Parsley Vine'.

***V. v.* 'Purpurea'**   This has young leaves of a rich claret red. The more mature leaves are a deep red-purple.

Vines on trees are usually left to their own devices. Those on pergolas or walls that are accessible, with the aid of a ladder, should have their long, new shoots shortened in the summer and pruned hard back to the main stem in winter. They can be encouraged to spread laterally by pruning during the growing season.

Interestingly enough, the vine and the common hop were among the first climbing plants to be grown by man.

WATTAKAKA Asclepiadaceae

W. sinensis   A twining evergreen, growing to about 2–3m (6.5–10ft). It has pairs of heart-shaped leaves to 10cm (4in) long points and these are densely velvety beneath. The fragrant hoya-like flowers are white and carried on long stalks. Each flower is about 1cm (0.4in) wide with five white, red-speckled petals. In most parts of the country, this needs a well sheltered site, preferably on a south west wall. Otherwise, it is an excellent climber for the cool greenhouse or conservatory. I have seen it grown in a largish suburban garden in Hertfordshire where it was flowering out of doors.

Cultural Notes   Needs a well-drained fertile soil. Propagate by cuttings in late summer. It is wise to take precautions so as not to allow the sap to enter the eyes as this is a persistent irri-tant. Do not rub the eyes with fingers that have handled the cuttings.

W. s. 'Variegata'   I am fortunate enough to have a plant that was the result of a mutant seedling and has leaves splashed with creamy-white. Thus, for me, the leaves have this added attraction.

WISTERIA Leguminosae

Wisterias, climbing roses, clematis and honey-suckles are perhaps the best known and loved climbing plants in Great Britain. Although there are ten or more species, only three are in wide cultivation. On mature, well-grown specimens, the flowers hang in racemes in a profusion of usually pale mauve scented blossoms.

W. floribunda   This is the Japanese wisteria and can achieve 10m (33ft) or more in growth. The leaves, composed of 13–19 leaflets, each 4–8cm (2–3in) long, are of a good lustrous green. The long flower racemes, often up to 25cm (9in) long, are of a good purple-blue colour in early sum-mer. The stems twine clockwise and it differs

Fig 62   A well-trained and pruned Wisteria in spring.

markedly from *W. sinensis* which twines anti-clockwise.

W.f. 'Alba'   This has white flowers.

W.f. 'Rosea'   Flowers are rose pink.

W.f. 'Violacea Plena'   Violet-purple, double flowered.

W. sinensis   The most widely grown of all wisterias. This is a strong growing species and can reach 18m (60ft). As has already been said, it twines anticlockwise and whilst having similar leaves to *W. floribunda*, its fragrant, flowering

Fig 63   *Arches of iron or wood in a rustic style are easily constructed over which climbers can be trained to great effect. Remember to make the width between the uprights wide enough when there are plants trained over them to allow for ease of passage.*

Fig 64   *Laburnum is part of the* Leguminosae *family, as is wisteria.*

racemes are 30cm (1ft) in length. Because of the length of these racemes, it is best grown and trained up a high wall or over a pergola, archway or other structure that is of ample strength in construction so that the long tresses of flowers can hang free to look their best. Other colour forms of *W. sinensis* are 'Alba' with white flowers, 'Black Dragon' has dark purple double flowers and 'Prolific' is an especially free-blooming clone. *W. sinensis* differs from *W. floribunda* in that all the flowers open more or less simultaneously.

W. venusta   This is a less common species and not as vigorous in growth as those previously mentioned. The larger white flowers on shorter racemes are slightly fragrant and come into bloom after *W. sinensis* has finished flowering. *W. venusta* is perhaps the best of the white flowered wisterias.

79

CLEMATIS

Clematis were introduced to England a little more than 200 years ago. *Clematis vitalba*, the 'Traveller's Joy' or 'Old Man's Beard' was the exception. This was known and recorded in this country before the sixteenth century.

One of the first introductions was *Clematis viticella* with its purple, saucer-shaped flowers. It used to be called 'The Virgin's Bower' and such tribute is said to be to the Virgin Queen, Elizabeth I, but others think the origin of the name honoured the Virgin Mary.

Clematis flammula, *coerulea* and *integrifolia* were amongst the first of many species to arrive in England, brought to our shores by sailors and explorers during the Elizabethan era, together with many other unusual plants introduced to England at this time. Most varieties are from the temperate regions of the world.

It was in the nineteenth century that the nurserymen of the day bred and crossed the species to produce many interesting hybrids and from these crosses, the famous 'Jackmanii' first flowered towards the end of the 1800s. This is possibly the best loved clematis and it is still very popular today. So many different forms of this queen of climbers are available with their diverse colours and shapes that we can enjoy their great beauty in all forms. They can be chosen to flower in spring, summer or autumn. The colour range is from purest white in double and single forms, good rich yellows, through plum red, deep purple, and the palest of pinks to deep blue.

Queen of Climbers

Clematis are undoubtedly the aristocrat of climbers and their colour, form and flowering period guarantees their inclusion in even the smallest of gardens. They are normally divided into three groups. The early flowering species and their hybrids are *C. alpina*, *C. macropetala* and *C. montana*. Next we have the summer flowering cultivars represented by the well known *C.* 'Nelly Moser'. Lastly, the later flower-ing group which is dominated by *C.* 'Jackmanii' and its many relatives and also includes the more vigorous growing species such as *C. orientalis*, *C. tangutica* and *C. viticella* as well as the her-baceous types which are low growing and can be seen to advantage in the flower border, though these sometimes need a little assistance by staking.

Clematis can be found in all of the usual flower colours, however, a good deep yellow is yet to be bred in the large summer flowering hybrids. Yellow is however, well represented in the later, small flowering species such as *C. orientalis* and *C. tangutica*. Many of the actual flower colours change quite noticeably in the life span of an in-dividual flower particularly when grown in full sun. The intense colours or the more delicate ones last longer if the plants are given a north facing situation. Many clematis seed heads are of great ornamental value and are highly prized by flower arrangers, in particular, *C. flammula*, *C. tangutica* and *C. orientalis*.

A few clematis are scented, for example *C. montana* 'Elizabeth'. A large and mature plant can produce a strongly perfumed area from its hundreds of pale pink flowers that fill the air with their fragrance. *C. flammula* has a vanilla scent and *C. rehderiana* has a perfume somewhat resembling cowslips.

Some cultivars have double flowers but they will also produce single flowers on young plants or when flowers appear after the normal flower-ing period. On the summer flowering hybrids that are particularly noted for their double flowers, such flowers are produced on the previous season's wood and single flowers ap-pear on the current season's growth. A recently introduced *C. montana* 'Marjorie' is both colour-ful and semi-double. The creamy pink sepals have a centre of salmon pink and are streaked with a darker pink.

Fig 65   Right: Clematis florida *'Sieboldii'*
(florida bicolour).

Planting

Clematis will grow in practically any soil and for those of you who garden on a limey soil, this is the plant for you. They like a deep root run. It is essential to break up the soil to a depth of at least 0.5m (1.5ft), deeper if possible, and add a mixture of peat and leaf compost and some well rotted compost or farm manure as clematis are gross feeders. If farmyard manure is not available, hop manure can be used plus bone meal, a slow acting fertiliser, which should be scattered around each plant in the autumn and generally carefully worked in. Be careful not to damage the roots with too deep a forking in of this bone meal. Clematis like a moist but well drained soil though like most plants, it resents a wet stagnant soil. So, ensure that there is plenty of drainage, use broken pots, brick or 2cm (0.8in) sized stones beneath the root ball.

As I have said in the general section on planting, it is wise to plant 30cm (1ft) or so from the wall and train the plant back to the trellis or wire. It is a good idea to peg the growing stem down to the ground between the main stem and the wall — roots will then form on this laid down or pegged in stem.

Most clematis plants are sent out by nurseries pot grown and certainly this is the way in which you will find them in garden centres. It is better to plant a little deeper than the pot level, for roots will always form on a portion of the stem below the ground — this being to the plant's advantage. The plant, knocked out of its pot, will often show you that the roots have curled round and round inside the pot. Tease out the lowest roots so that you can spread them evenly around the root ball in the hole. This may take a little time and patience. Place your plant carefully in the soil at the bottom of the hole, leaving the cane in position and gently fill in, making the soil firm by gently treading around the plant.

The stem of a young clematis is very fragile. It is a good idea to place a cylinder of wire netting around the base of the plant of about 30cm (1ft) high and let this netting into the soil 3cm (1in) or

so. Two or three canes will support the wire netting until the plant is established.

A hot, dry soil is fatal to clematis, for they like a cool, moist root run. Bedding plants or small shrubs can be used in front of and around clematis or even a stone slab, tiles or crazy paving, for underneath these it is usually cool and moist. Remember, these plants like their feet in the shade and their heads in the sun. Large pebbles scattered thickly around the base of the plant are also very effective. Rain can then soak through and the pebbles look neat and tidy.

Pruning Clematis – The First Year

For a first year plant, that is one that you have newly planted, remember during the first spring and summer to prune hard and prune often. You may see some lovely plump buds at the top of the cane but steel yourself, cut the stem well below down to a few centimetres if possible. You will see two buds forming on the stem at the base and these will probably not be as forward as those that you have just cut off. It is these buds that will make the well trained plant of the future.

A dressing of sulphate of potash can be given in March, it promotes strong growth and is good for colour in foliage and flower. Apply two ounces to a square yard, sprinkling the powder around the plant and watering well in. During late spring, two strong shoots should develop from the two buds that the clematis has been cut down to, although sometimes one of these buds will remain dormant and only one shoot will appear. When these shoots on the plant 'break' and are about 15–20cm (6–8in) long and have two pairs of leaf buds on them, cut back again to the topmost leaf bud which means just nipping out the growing tip, between two fingers. This encourages the plant to 'break' again and become well furnished and bushy at the base.

Every shoot that appears should be stopped or pruned after it has made a strong start of about 30cm (1ft). Do not despair if one shoot accidentally breaks off or the wind batters the plant and damages one or more shoots. Nature

Fig 66   Clematis florida 'Plena'

Fig 67   Clematis viticella 'Kermesina', bright colour, very effective and prolific.

will soon send out more shoots to give a fine specimen plant in the future.

Another good reason for this continued stopping during the first year is that hard pruning helps to ward off the mysterious complaint from which clematis suffer – clematis wilt. This disease usually attacks in the first year or two in the life of a clematis. Rarely, if ever, does the well established plant die from this wilt. If it does occur in a plant that has been well furnished with strong shoots in its first year, it will be capable of resisting an attack by re-growing from the base. The collapse is more often than not caused by allowing too much top growth in a young plant. The roots are really unable to support excessive top growth and the plant fails before it has had a chance to establish itself. Clematis hate being dry at the roots and this is another reason for failure early in life. You cannot over water clematis. A tablespoon of one of the proprietary liquid manures to a bucket of water will help to feed as well as water your plant. By July, your plant should be well established. Stop the pruning and, with luck, you will get a few flowers on the young wood in September. Your young plant will have had a good start in life and should give a fine display of magnificent blooms the following year.

Most nurseries sell only young plants and so one must not expect a mass of bloom for the first year or two. It may be possible to obtain 2–3 year old plants in pots but these are certainly more expensive. Should you find these, it will save at least a year or two of waiting and help to give a display immediately in the year of planting.

Pruning Clematis in Subsequent Years

To some, one of the greatest mysteries and stumbling blocks in growing clematis successfully is their correct pruning. As a general rule, prune all late flowering varieties hard, but those that bloom early, leave alone but just tidy the plant to the area that you wish to cover. The following groupings will help you to choose those that need pruning.

GROUP A Spring flowering species, hybrids and cultivars. Prune only if space is limited, cutting out all shoots that have flowered immediately after flowering.
Clematis alpina, macropetala, armandii, montana and chrysocoma.

GROUP B These are usually the large flowered hybrids that start their main flush of bloom before mid-June. In February and March, you should shorten all vines to the first pair of strong buds, cutting out all dead growth.

GROUP C These are the clematis that flower after June and possibly as late as September. These are the small flowered species clematis.
Clematis viticella, rehderiana, flammula, tangutica, the hybrid Jackmanii and the hybrids of texensis. In late February to March, cut all growth hard back to one metre or less above ground level. This will entail the removal of many healthy looking green shoots, but do not let this deter you. This method applies to all later flowering clematis.

If this guide is taken as a quick rule of thumb, you should be reasonably successful with your pruning, though some of the hybrids of Group B can slot into Group C and benefit from hard pruning. All you have to do is to find out when your plant blooms normally. If it is an early bloomer, do not prune. If it flowers late, from July onwards, then prune hard every year, preferably in February. Many people like to have a tidy garden and this hard pruning can be carried out in the late autumn.

Training and Trellis

Clematis climb by twining their leaves tightly around anything available, one has only to pro-

Fig 68   Clematis x durandii.

vide the support and the plant will do the rest. Trellis fixed to the wall is an excellent method, or plastic wire with vine eyes screwed into the wall at intervals is also very efficient. Stretch the wire to make a pattern of 15–20cm (6–8in) squares using wall nails or vine eyes to hold the wire firmly at the top, bottom and sides. The wire should be kept at least 2cm (0.8in) from the wall so that the plant can weave its way through. If it is necessary to decorate the wall or carry out repairs, clematis can be readily pruned back and the wire taken off and replaced with new. The clematis will then grow up again quite happily.

Posts and pillars are also effective means of support. Clematis can also be grown along the ground, by training over wire netting or pea sticks and by pegging to the ground. The Jackmanii types are the best for this purpose for they flower for three months or so and thus

Fig 69   The hole should be prepared away from the overhang of any branches. Fill the hole with well enriched top soil and the young plant should have a good start in life. Remember to keep the planting area well watered until the plant is fully established. This site is ideal for clematis and other climbers that are intended to ramble through larger trees and shrubs.

provide a more or less permanent bedding plant. Underplanted with small bulbs, the clematis will help to hide the dying leaves of the bulbs in the late spring.

Some gardening writers advocate the 'tying in' of clematis. This I practise on the young growths but I do it very loosely, ensuring that the plant ties, raffia or plastic fillis is not tied too tightly round the clematis and the cane or wire as this could easily damage the growing stem. Make a loop with your tie of about 1cm (0.4in) in diameter, thus giving the clematis sufficient room to move about and grow on within this circle.

CLEMATIS Ranunculaceae – a recommended selection

Varieties and species of clematis can be chosen to give an astonishingly long flowering season.
In April *C. armandii*, *C. alpina*, *C. macropetala* and their varieties are at their best. The many forms of *C. montana* are going through their flowering season in May. By the end of May, the large flowered hybrids are coming into their own with their display, together with those forms which have enormous double flowers. These often flower again later on young wood and have single flowers.

At the end of June and the beginning of July, the varieties that flower on the current year's growth begin to flower such as *C. viticella*, *C.* jackmanii hybrids, *C. tangutica* and *C. texensis*. Their flowering season will variously go right through to the end of September.

Spring Flowering

This hardy group have flowers like nodding lanterns and open during April. These are followed by gorgeous, fluffy seed heads. Odd flowers are produced during summer months.

C. alpina   Nodding blue flowers.

C. a. 'Frances Rivis'   The blue flowers are extra large.

C. a. 'Ruby'   Bears purplish-pink flowers.

C. a. 'White Moth'   The flowers are double white.

C. a. sibirica   A white flowered form.

C. macropetala flower during April and early May and generally have lavender blue, semi-double, nodding flowers with occasional summer flowers later in the year. There are other colour forms now available. Again, this species have superb fluffy seed heads. This clematis will grow well if planted in a north facing postion and can be successfully grown in a large container or tub.

C. macropetala   Soft, lavender blue, semi-double flowers.

C. m. 'Maidwell Hall'   Flowers are a deep blue.

C. m. 'Markham's Pink'   Lavender pink flowers with white stamens.

C. m. 'Snowbird'   A slightly later flowering form with white flowers.

C. montana   The 5cm (2in) white flowers have a vanilla scent.

C. m. 'Elizabeth'   Soft pink flowers.

C. m. 'Picton's Variety'   Flowers of a deeper pink.

C. m. rubens   Pale, mauve-pink flowers with dark green foliage.

C. m. 'Tetrarose'   8–9cm (3–3.5in) flowers are a deep rosy-mauve. Good bronze-green foliage.

C. m. 'Marjorie'   A recent introduction with semi-double flowers. Sepals are creamy-pink with a salmon-pink sepaloid boss at the flower centre around the stamens.

Early Flowering Hybrids

Many of these carry 15–20cm (6–8in) diameter flowers on the previous year's ripened wood. The flowers tend to appear in a flush and the general effect is dramatic. They flower for 4–6 weeks from early May to the middle of June. Some give a secondary flowering on young wood but these blooms are often smaller. There are so many different colours and shapes of flowers to choose from that to give a recommended list is very difficult as each reader will have a different preference. Therefore, they are best seen in flower at the nursery to make your selection. However, do remember that the lighter coloured flowers or the more delicate shades are best planted on a north facing wall or similar structure.

'Nelly Moser'   Is a must for it is one of the older and more trusted varieties and certainly needs a north wall or the colour of the flowers will fade.

'Duchess of Edinburgh'   If you like double or semi-double flowers this has large white double flowers with many sepals and creamy anthers. However, these can become very sad looking in a wet season.

'Jackmanii Rubra'   Occasional double flowers of a deep crimson with creamy yellow anthers.

'Kathleen Dunford'   Rosy-purple double flowers.

'Proteus'   Flowers of a soft mauve pink with the sepals darker at the margins.

'Vyvyan Pennell'   Double clematis with lilac outer sepals and a lavender blue central rosette. The anthers are creamy yellow.

There will be many other good double flowered forms to choose from at your nursery or garden centre.

Mid-Season Large Flowered Cultivars

These flower intermittently on the previous year's ripened wood through the summer until the first autumn frosts. They grow best when planted where their open habit can run riot through a large shrub, displaying their flowers over their host. A selection of the best to look for at your nursery are:

'Henryi'   Pure white flowers with dark stamens.

'Marie Boisselot' (Madame Le Coultre)   Large, pure white flowers of overlapping sepals and yellow stamens. Long flowering period.

'Sealand Gem'   Rosy-mauve flowers with a deeper bar and brown stamens. The sepals are wavy. It is very free flowering.

'The President'   Flowers of a deep purple-blue with reddish-purple stamens. Long flowering season.

'W E Gladstone'   This has possibly the largest flowers of all in this group. The flowers are lilac-blue with purple stamens.

Late Flowering Cultivars

These varieties all bloom on the current season's growth and need hard pruning every winter or at least before the middle of February. Most varieties need a sunny aspect and will do equally well on an east, south or west wall.

'Comtesse de Bouchaud'   The 12–15cm (4.5–6in) flowers are bright mauve-pink and are produced in great profusion.

'Ernest Markham'   Striking red flowers with oblong sepals of vivid magenta and chocolate anthers.

'Jackmanii Superba'   Dark, velvety-purple flowers 12cm (4.5in) in size, produced in quantity.

'Madame Edouard André'   Medium sized flowers of dusky red with yellow anthers.

'Rouge Cardinal'   A slender grower with velvety crimson flowers and brown anthers.

'Niobe'   Deep ruby red flowers, almost black when first opening. Golden stamens.

'Huldine'   Small, pearly white flowers with a mauve bar on the reverse. Pale yellow stamens.

Fig 70 Clematis 'Comtesse de Bouchaud'. This has beautifully ruffled sepals with a golden boss.

Again, there are so many to choose from that they are best researched when in flower at the nursery or garden centre as each of us have our own preferences to colour and form.

The Viticella Group

These smaller flowered clematis flower on the current season's growth and are quite vigorous. They will easily top a fence or trellis. The growths then continue and hang over the top of their support.

'Alba Luxurians' A mass of creamy-white, smallish flowers with green tipped sepals which twist. Dark anthers.

'Etoile Violette' Medium sized violet flowers with creamy anthers.

'Purpurea Plena Elegans' This is a very old double form which produces an abundance of tight rosette-like flowers with violet sepals which appear continuously from July through until September.

Fig 71   Clematis viticella *'Purpurea Plena Elegans'.*

'Royal Velours'   Very deep, velvety purple sepals and should be grown against a light background to be seen to the best advantage.

'Rubra'   The flowers are wine-red with dark centres.

Again, I recommend that you see this group of clematis in flower at your nursery, they are all beautiful.

Late Flowering Species

This range of clematis and its hybrids are vigorous and most useful for growing through trees and very large shrubs, or on unsightly walls and out-buildings. All produce their flowers on the new or current season's growth. Treat as *viticella* types in that they should be pruned back by reducing all stems to within 30cm (1ft) above ground in February to March. As I have said in my

90

comments on the previous groupings of clematis, it is best to choose them in flower at your nursery as descriptions do not always do their flowers justice.

C. x 'Huldine'   A must and an excellent variety with growths each year of 5–6m (16–20ft). Flowering is from July till September with white flowers above which are mauve beneath.

C. orientalis 'Bill MacKenzie'   The largest flowering form of the orientalis group. The yellow bell-shaped flowers are followed by lovely fluffy seed heads.

C. orientalis 'L & S 13342'   This is the seed collector's number when seed was brought back from Tibet. It has very finely cut foliage and a long flowering season of deep yellow bell-like flowers, with each sepal being as thick as orange peel. Hence its name of 'The Orange Peel Clematis'.

Fig 72   Clematis orientalis.

Fig 73   Close-up view of Clematis orientalis.

Fig 74   Newly-formed seedheads on Clematis orientalis.

C. tangutica   Yellow, lantern-shaped flowers on annual growth stems of 5–6m (16–20ft). Flowers July till September and has very fine seed heads.

C. texensis 'Gravetye Beauty'   A hybrid of a scarlet flowered clematis, the true species originating from Texas. The flowers are held erect and resemble small, deep red tulips which gradually open into star shaped flowers of 4–5 sepals. This is ideal for training over low growing shrubs. There are other hybrids in the *texensis* group that are worth seeking out. All require extra good rich soil and a warm, sunny wall.

C. rehderiana   A vigorous species from Western China. It has loose clusters of dull yellow bell-shaped flowers and a delightful perfume of cowslips. Flowers from September to October and is ideal for growing through a large tree.

Herbaceous and Semi-Herbaceous Types

Pruning consists of removing all top growth as soon as the plant has died down to the ground from November onwards.

C. heracleifolia   This is a sub shrub from China and has pale blue, hyacinth-like flowers on long, woody stems.

Hybrids of heracleifolia are:

C. h. davidiana   This has deep blue flowers on woody stems of 1m (3.3ft) high.

'Wyevale'   A form which produces even larger flowers of a deep blue in August–September. These flowers are fragrant.

C. integrifolia   This form has nodding indigo-blue flowers in clusters of twos and threes. It needs tying to a stake as it tends to be lax in growth; alternatively it can be grown as a scrambler through a shrub.

'Olgae'   This has sepals of a clear pale blue.

'Rosea'   The sepals are a rich pink.

Clematis recta   Another herbaceous species with matt foliage and has a crowd of small white blossoms at the end of 1.5–2m (5–6.5ft) woody growths. Needs staking.

'Purpurea'   Try to find this form which has foliage of a purple-bronze colouring early in the year on the new growth. Flowers June to July which are the same small white blossoms as the above.

A Few Reminders on the Cultivation of Clematis

The colour of clematis flowers can vary as each individual bloom lasts often for three weeks and there is a slight change in colour from the first day that it opens, being darker than was first expected, settling down to its true colour and gradually fading towards the end of its flowering period. To keep the paler and more subtle colours from fading, it is best to plant them on a north facing wall.

Fig 75   Clematis x durandii.

Clematis will give a fantastic display of flowers every year, providing that they are given some help.

A good mulching of farmyard manure every autumn is desirable. If this is unobtainable, then a top dressing of peat, having worked in three good handfuls of bone meal around the stem in November is a suitable alternative. Further, a handful of sulphate of potash sprinkled around the stem in the spring will help to keep the clematis healthy and the flowers in good colour.

A good soaking during the summer with water two or three times a week is essential. Once a week, include in the water a liquid fertiliser. Remember that clematis are gross feeders.

Plant deep, that is, at least one pair of buds at the base of the stem should be buried, thus allowing several stems to develop from below the ground.

Slugs and snails can be troublesome to young plants, eating the tender shoots at ground level. Control by using slug pellets or using your own favourite remedy for these garden pests.

IVIES

The common ivy, *Hedera helix*, is so much part of our environment, growing as it does in woodland, hedgerows and on buildings, that many do not appreciate its merits in the garden. It is known over the greater part of the world, though thought of as a typically British plant.

From earliest times, ivy has been a familiar plant in Europe. In mythology, it was associated with Bacchus and Bacchanalian orgies. It is also associated with pagan practices and has been incorporated into Christian ritual. As old Christmas carols remind us, ivy became a traditional Christmas decoration together with holly. From the time of Chaucer and until well into the Middle Ages, a 'bush' of ivy hung on a pole indicated a tavern. This custom, it is said, came from the Romans and spread throughout Europe. The sign was called an ale pole or alestake and is mentioned in the Canterbury Tales. From this we obtained the phrase 'good wine needs no bush' meaning that a good product needs no advertisement. There are records of ivy plants living well into a ripe old age of 300 years or more.

Whilst ivy as referred to above was the common ivy, *Hedera helix*, there are other species of ivy belonging to the genus *Hedera* hailing from other parts of the old world, with distribution extending from Japan in the East to the Azores in the West and from Northern Europe to North Africa. Ivy is not naturally present in the Americas or in Australasia. These other species are *Hedera canariensis*, *colchica*, *nepalensis*, *pastuchovii* and *rhombea*. Modern botanists have recently named two other species namely, *H. azorica* and *H. algeriensis*.

Over the years horticulturists have selected individual plants from the wild and these have

Fig 76   The flowers of ivy, so loved by bees in the late season.

Fig 77 Ivy can soften a harsh chain fence.

been named and propagated vegetatively. Such a clone is usually raised from a stem that has sported or mutated and has undergone change in the arrangement of the cells that govern colour or form. There are 400 different recognised and officially named varieties with an amazing range of leaf shape and colour. Many of the colours change throughout the seasons and with the age of the plant.

Leaf shapes can take many forms such as crenate, dentate, entire or lobed. Colouring can range through many shades of green, bronze-black and purple in winter months, a glorious golden yellow in sunlight with variegations of green and yellow, green and white and there are variegated patterns which appear as blotching, spotting or marbling.

Ivies are very adaptable, they have an ability to survive and even thrive in almost any type of soil and are therefore a useful and easy plant to grow. The plant is most interesting for its dimorphus growth habit. A botanical dictionary tells us that this means 'having two distinct forms in the one plant'. In its juvenile form, the ivy is non-flowering, it creeps and climbs by adhesive rootlets and the leaves are arranged on one plane in two rows. They are palmately lobed, with veins appearing silvery-white against the often shiny, dark green, leathery background of the upper leaf surface.

Once the juvenile ivy has reached the top of its support and thereby arrived at a position with the brightest light, its growth characteristics change significantly. It continues to grow, produc-

ing stems with leaves arranged all around the stem. These leaves however, are invariably elliptical in shape and without lobes. The white colouring is usually absent from the veins and the leaves appear all green. These adult shoots do not produce clinging rootlets and are eventually topped with umbels of flowers.

A well furnished ivy plant with these adult growths, all terminating in flowers from September, is a sight worth seeing and often not understood by the casual observer. These ivy flowers are much appreciated by bees and wasps for the late season nectar. The flowers are yellowish-green with five sepals, five petals, five stamens and a five celled ovary, and grow in a round inflorescence of 2–3cm (0.8– 1in) according to the species.

The insects are attracted by an abundance of nectar secreted by a yellowish disk located at the base of the stamens. The insects brush the anthers and they, having released their pollen, quickly drop and the stigma becomes receptive to pollen from other flowers. The resultant berries are green during the winter and ripen by May and June the following year when they turn a bluish-black.

The reasons for dimorphism are not fully understood, but one can assume that a wide-lobed leaf is more efficient in catching the light necessary for photosynthesis for a plant which is creeping along the forest floor or is within the darkened interior of a hedgerow. When it ascends and finds better light and air which seem necessary for it to flower, it is then able to change

Fig 78 A good use of ivy to soften brickwork of an archway.

whilst the climbing or juvenile growth cuttings of 2–3 nodes root readily in two weeks in a suitable propagating medium and within a closed frame, 15cm (6in) cuttings of the arborescent or tree ivy with the flowering umbel pinched out and removed, invariably need the addition of a rooting hormone and patience for six months or more for a cutting to have sufficient roots to enable it to be potted up. The successful production of well rooted arborescent growths is a tribute to the propagator.

The Myth of Ivy Damage to Walls

It is as well at this point, to assure readers and to dispel any of those handed-down myths that ivies should not be grown on the walls of a house because of the damage that they do to the structure.

The truth is the very opposite. Providing that the brickwork is structurally sound, walls clad with ivy are dry and warm, and it acts as an insulator against winds, frost, cold and rain. So much so that householders in Germany are encouraged to grow ivy on their houses for insulation. However, it is necessary to hard prune ivy to control its vigorous growth penetrating between roof tiles and slates and clogging gutters and drain-pipes.

On masonry or brick walls of great age, constructed using a soft mortar of sand and lime, I have seen erosion and instability of the uppermost part of these walls that were covered with ivy. I have concluded, after seeing very many walls constructed in this manner, that the damage has been caused more by the neglect of the ivy, by allowing it to grow into a tangled mass, invariably with arborescent growth, and by letting it become top heavy. During heavy winds, much buffeting of this cumbersome bushy mass had loosened the topmost structure, and, being constructed with a lime-based mortar, the 'bond' between the brick or stone and the mortar had become weakened. In the more modern structures using cement-based mortars, the 'bond' is considerably stronger and further-

its growth habit to produce flowers and so attract the flies upon which the plant depends for fertilisation, thus perpetuating the species. Possibly too, during the course of evolution, a narrower unlobed leaf became better adapted to survive any drought conditions that may occur than would a wider lobed leaf.

The plant's dimorphic habit has a bonus for if cuttings are taken from the flowering shoots, they keep the adult leaf character and the arborescent habit and can grow into substantial self supporting bushes. These have been known in the past as tree ivies.

The variegated clones were used quite extensively in Victorian garden plantings. However,

Fig 79   A variegated ivy starting its ascent to soften the hard outlines of a brick wall.

either old or damaged enough to let light into the top of the tree. Generally, the shade cast by the crown of a healthy tree will confine the ivy to the trunk and lower limbs. The tree will continue to flourish even though it is hosting a green covering of ivy on its lower trunk.

It is only when the canopy of seasonal leaves on a dying tree is non-existent that the ivy see its opportunity and rapidly climbs into the light. With the increase of sunlight, the ivy rapidly engulfs its host, so giving the impression that it has killed the tree.

It is sometimes suggested that trees are strangled by the ivy. This so-called constriction is not nearly so damaging as that produced by honeysuckles or similar climbers of an even more twining habit.

Furthermore, contrary to very widespread and popular belief, ivy is not a parasite. It does not live off the tree upon which it grows but only uses it as a support. Many think that the thousands of aerial root-like hairs by which it clings to the tree are feeding roots. This can easily be disproved by cutting the ivy stems at their base whereupon the climbing stems will quickly die.

There is nothing quite like a mature planting of ivy for attracting wildlife into the garden. For those with an interest in conservation, in late summer the nectar-rich blossoms of ivy attract bees, hoverflies and wasps. The resulting crop of bluish-black berries feed many different types of birds and the evergreen growth will give them much shelter and protection. There is also strong competition in the spring for nesting sites amidst the dense foliage with wrens, greenfinches, thrushes and blackbirds being the most regular tenants.

I hope that the reader will forgive my rather long defence of ivy for I am firmly committed to praising it as an attractive, all year round, reliable and hardy evergreen. Ivy is a wonderful plant for softening outlines of structures and clothing fences, outbuildings, sheds and walls and there are many leaf shapes and colourings from which to choose.

more, waterproof and it can therefore withstand to a considerably greater extent the weight of the top heavy growth.

I have also observed in ruins of houses and castles with walls of great age, that often the walls covered with ivy were in a far better condition and were dry compared to the walls without ivy growth. The walls that were without this growth had crumbled, due to the ravages of time and the elements.

In Further Defence of Ivy

Some people contend that ivy kills trees. This rarely happens and usually only when the tree is

A Selected List of Ivies Suitable for Clothing Structures

Hedera canariensis
(The Canary Island Ivy)

H. c. 'Gloire de Marengo'   The glossy leaves are irregularly marked dark green and silvery-grey with a creamy-white border. The leaf size is 9–11cm (3.5–4in) across and is also as much from the tip to the point of attachment of the petiole – the leaf stalk, which is of a lovely wine-red colour as are the young climbing stems of this ivy.

H. c. 'Montgomery'   This is an all-green clone with leaves that are considerably broader than those of the above. This ivy again has the lovely red stems and petioles and is a good climber. It is unusual and will probably need to be obtained from one of the specialist ivy nurseries. In the winter, these dark green leaves turn darker, almost to black with reddish hues.

H. c. 'Ravensholst'   This is a very similar ivy to the above with dark green leaves and can be quite vigorous.

Hedera colchica
(The Persian Ivy)

This has large, generally unlobed, heart-shaped leaves 8–13cm (3–5in) by 8cm (3in) or more and are usually somewhat matt green on the upper surface and with green stems. In America, this has come to be called 'My Heart' ivy because of its leaf shape. It is an extremely hardy species showing little damage to the leaves in even very cold winters.

H. c. 'Dentata'   This is the form that has even larger leaves, anything up to 20cm (8in) by 17cm (7in) and they can be, in good growing conditions, up to 25cm (9in) across and as long. However, unlike the previous colchicas, the heart-shaped leaves are broken by widely spaced fine 'teeth'. In mature specimens, the leaves tend to hang down with the older leaves curling at the edges. A strong and vigorous ivy for a wall.

Fig 80   Hedera colchica *'Dentata Variegata', a large leaved ivy making an excellent cover for a low wall.*

Fig 81   The large leaved ivy Hedera colchica *'Sulphur Heart'*.

H. c. 'Dentata Variegata'   This ivy is most spectacular and is probably one of the most showy evergreen climbers of all the hardy ivies. The green, leathery textured, matt surfaced leaves are broken by irregular patches of grey-green and they have an irregular leaf margin of a deep creamy-yellow. These variegated leaves are only slightly smaller than the form mentioned above.

H. c. 'Sulphur Heart'   No less showy and hardy than the above and equally vigorous. The shiny, roughly heart-shaped leaves are of a light green colour with bold, irregular splashes of yellow in the central area. This ivy is a stunner with its great pendant, handkerchief sized leaves. It needs a little tying in to help it to climb up its support as it seldom affixes itself with adventitious rootlets. This ivy is sometimes offered as 'Paddy's Pride'.

Hedera helix

This is the native English ivy and generally has leaves smaller than the *canariensis* and *colchica* ivies described above. With the naming of modern selections of the common ivy of our hedgerows, leaves can be from as little as 1.5cm (0.5in) by 2cm (0.8in) to as much as 7–8cm (2.5–3in) long and as wide. *Hedera helix* is extremely hardy as are many of the selected clones. The diverse shapes of the leaves and their colourings are from green, through clear yellow, to combinations of yellow, green and white, and through winter colours of reds, purples and blacks. The following selections are ideally suitable for climbing, though naturally, they can be used in many instances to hang down over low walls or used as ground cover. For a wider selection and descriptions, I advise the reader to seek the catalogues of specialist ivy nurserymen for the choice in their listings can stretch to over 300 different named clones.

***H. h.* 'Adam'**   A self branching ivy with quite small, tri-lobed leaves of 3–4cm (1–1.5in). These leaves have a white-cream edging with a light green centre.

***H. h.* 'Angularis Aurea'**   This is an old ivy with 3-lobed, 4–5cm (1.5–2in) leaves which are glossy green, suffused with yellow. This yellow colour is more prominent in sunlight during the spring. Later in the year, the leaves become mottled and can become wholly green. This ivy provides a splendid covering for a wall or fence, giving the impression in that part of the garden, that the sun is shining, even on a dull day.

***H. h.* 'Anna Marie'**   A most attractive ivy with 5–6cm (2–2.5in) leaves somewhat wider than long. They have a grey-green centre and a clear cream variegation at the leaf edge.

***H. h.* 'Atropurpurea'**   This ivy can be offered by nurserymen as 'Purpurea' or 'Nigra'. In the summer, this has dark green 5-lobed leaves and the winter months produce a colouring of a deep purple, depending upon its exposure to cold weather.

***H. h.* 'Buttercup'**   A must for any garden, this ivy is a superb trailer for a low wall, as a scrambler over dark-leaved shrubs, over trellis and arbours or as a climber. The leaves are 5-lobed, 5–7cm (2–2.8in) in size and in good light

Fig 82   Hedera helix 'Buttercup', the two-coloured leaves of this ivy make an excellent close mat of ground cover, particularly effective in suppressing weeds.

and in sun, are a good golden yellow. In shade, the leaves are a light green.

H. h. **'California Fan'**   The leaves are of a light green, 5–7 lobed with the lobes bluntly acute and pointing forward and in a fan-like shape.

H. h. **'Chester'**   An ivy that I would not want to be without in the garden. Of recent introduction from Europe about ten years ago, it makes a compact, self branching plant with triangular leaves that are a soft lime green when young with a dark green centre. As the leaf ages, the lime green area changes with creamy-white margins to the leaves. It makes an excellent climber, is hardy and is always noticed by visitors.

H. h. **'Cockleshell'**   This is an ivy that was selected in America and, as the name implies, the leaves are concave with a slight ruffling on the upturned edges. The whole leaf is almost circular in outline and light green when young, maturing to a darker green. The plant is self branching and bushy.

H. h. **'Deltoidea'**   This is variously known as 'The Shield Ivy' in England and 'The Sweetheart Ivy' in America. The leaf outline is 3-lobed but so shallow that the resultant leaf is deltoid. The leaf base has overlapping lobes and is quite thick leaved for an ivy. Leaves are dark green, turning to dark purple in the autumn. I have known it to be called 'The Ox Heart Ivy' as, presumably, it resembles an ox heart with its winter colouring and leaf shape.

H. h. **'Eugen Hahn'**   The triangular, heart-shaped leaves are 3–5cm (1.5–2in) long with a cream base colour densely stippled and marbled with green, having a salt and pepper look. This ivy seldom seems to be offered by general nurserymen but is well worth a place in the garden. It throws long and strong vining trails and is therefore a good ivy for growing over dwarf walls as the growths will hang down well. With a little tying in, it will climb a wall.

H. h. **'Fantasia'**   The yellow-cream leaves are basically 5-lobed and are mottled and speckled with light and dark green. Some leaves can be all green and some almost white.

H. h. **'Fluffy Ruffles'**   An American ivy that has been in my collection for many years. I sought it out because of its name and was not disappointed. It is a distinctive, much branching ivy with leaves basically 5-lobed, but the edges are so curled and twisted as to appear that the leaf edges are frilled. Young leaves are yellow-green, the frilled edges often pink tinged. The colouring on these frills darkens as does the leaf with age.

H. h. **'Glacier'**   I doubt if the true 'Glacier' as selected by the original grower can be found in a nurseryman's stock today. This is a popular ivy and has thus been propagated by almost every nurseryman world wide. Many have not selected their propagating material to be in character with the given name. Hence, I now think of ivies under this name as 'The Glacier Group'. The leaves, when grown in the garden, are 3–5 lobed of roughly 3–5cm (1.5–2in) and are of a mixture of grey and green with lighter silver grey patches and a very thin cream rim. This ivy is entirely hardy and will throw variously shaped leaves with varying mixtures of colour.

H. h. **'Goldchild'**   A self-branching, 3-lobed ivy with leaves of 4–5cm (1.5–2in), the centre lobe quite wedge-shaped. It has a good yellow leaf margin surrounding a central area of grey-green. This was the first 'break' or sport to give ivy enthusiasts a yellow margined ivy. Mr Tom Rochford was very proud to show me the first five plants of this selection which occurred in Europe and of which he purchased the entire stock. This entrepreneurial nurseryman needed a catchy name to launch it at a forthcoming Chelsea Show. I had learned while being shown round his nursery, that on that day he had become a grandfather. I suggested that the ivy be called 'Goldchild' to which he readily agreed.

Fig 83 Hedera helix *'Goldheart' on a sunny wall.*

Fig 84 Hedera helix *'Goldheart' clothing a tree trunk.*

H. h. 'Goldheart' The leaves of this ivy are 3-lobed 4–6cm (I.5–2.5in) by 4–6cm (I.5–2.5in), the central lobe being the longer of the three. These leaves are a glossy green, irregularly splashed in the centre with a good yellow. This is a beginner's ivy if ever there was one and possibly now being over planted. Old plantings certainly look at their best when overhanging and straggly growths are clipped back annually. This prevents a bedraggled look that is so often seen where 'Goldheart' has climbed to the height of its support. The growths begin to bush out, hang down and make a tangled mass, blowing about willy-nilly in gusts of wind, to the point where the strong climbing shoots adhering to the wall or support in such an attractive pattern, become obscured by this overhanging tangle.

H. h. 'Manda's Crested' The light green, typically 5-lobed, star-shaped leaves have the basal lobes pointing backwards and overlapping, the lateral lobes curl backwards and across one another. Young leaves have a strong ruffled pink to red edge, suffused to the leaf centre. In sunlight in the spring, this colouring is most attractive. The mature leaf is quite large for a *helix* being 7–8cm (3–3.5in) across and as long.

H. h. 'Minor Marmorata' This is a long, vining ivy of considerable age with leaves that are

3-lobed, though sometimes 5-lobed. The base colour is dark green, which is spotted and splashed with creamy-white. Unfortunately, this ivy is sometimes sold as 'Salt and Pepper', 'Marmorata Minor' or 'Discolour', the latter being an early name from Victorian times. This ivy climbs well and most usefully, it is best for a north wall.

H. h. 'Parsley Crested'   This ivy is often offered as *H. h.* 'Cristata'. It has light green crinkly edged, rounded leaves of 4–6cm (1.5–2.5in) by 4–6cm (1.5–2.5in). It is an ivy that as often as not, needs some assistance to climb, otherwise it can be very lax and floppy.

H. h. 'Pedata'   This is a selection of an ivy from our hedgerows and has been recorded for over a century. As the name implies, the leaf is cut to resemble the foot of a bird. The leaf lobes are very long, pointed and narrow with the basal lobes pointing backwards, the other lobes pointing forwards. These leaves are grey-green. This ivy is ideal for walls or pillars to show its most attractive leaf pattern to the best advantage.

H. h. 'Spetchley'   This is possibly the smallest leaved ivy and has been called 'Minima' by nurserymen before the war. It is ideal for rockeries and most suitable for growing between paving stones. The leaves are 3-lobed, dark green and can be 0.5–2cm (0.3–0.8in) long. The centre lobe is quite elongated. For quite a small leaf, it has a thick texture, the stems are a lovely purple and there are purple petioles to the leaves.

Ivy is a plant of infinite variety. There are many, many more clones that are suitable for a garden in the *helix* species but most of these are really more suitable for a rock garden, pots, tubs and urns.

There are also the upright growing ivies, sometimes called 'Candlestick' ivies that make superb specimen plants.

Fig 85   Hedera helix 'Erecta'. *An example of the candelabra or candlestick ivy. This would make a good specimen plant in front of a bare stemmed climber.*

Hedera nepalensis
(The Himalayan Ivy)

H. n. 'Sinensis'   The leaves are ovate to lanceolate, 6–10cm (2.5–4in) long and 3cm (1in) or so wide. They are very obscurely lobed and are of a soft green colour with an interesting grey vein pattern. This ivy is a slow grower, but fun if you want to collect this species.

H. n. **'Suzanne'** This ivy is named after Suzanne Pierot, the founder of The American Ivy Society and who wrote a book entitled 'The Ivy Book'. This plant is a smaller version of the above, the leaves having more noticeable lobing and a rather pleasant pattern of light veins on the dark green leaves.

Hedera pastuchovii
(The Russian Ivy)

The narrowly ovate, 6cm (2.5in) long to 3cm (1in) wide leaves are dark glossy green with a quite thick and leathery texture. There is a good patterning of veining visible. Again, this is an ivy for the enthusiast.

Hedera rhombea
(The Japanese Ivy)

This is a delicate ivy with more or less unlobed, triangular leaves of 2–4cm (0.8–1.5in) long and 4cm (1.5in) wide. These leaves are of a medium green and of quite thick texture.

H. r. **'Variegata'** This ivy has similar leaves to the above but with a narrow and regular band of white to the edge. This plant takes time to become a well clothed specimen but always looks very neat with its purple stems and purple-green petioles. The arborescent form of this clone, when in flower, is most delicate and attractive.

Hedera azorica

The green leaved clone normally offered under this name has superb 5–7 lobed, 11cm by 12cm (4–4.5in) leaves when mature. The colour of the leaves is bright green with a matt appearance, which is due to the abundant hairs visible to the naked eye, above and below the leaves, and along the green petioles and more or less so along the green stems. Recently, a clone of *H. azorica*, with more of a cut leaf and having deep sinuses between the lobes, is now passing around among collectors.

H. a. **'Variegata'** This plant has been known in Europe, possibly as far back to the last century. It is a poor 'doer' in the garden and very slow growing. The leaves are variously marked with a green centre and an irregular creamy-white margin. Other leaves on the same plant can be either all green with white blotching and streaks. Again, this ivy is hairy and has certainly proved to be hardy during the thirty years or so that I have grown it. It is a very difficult ivy to propagate. It has been known on the Continent in early writings as *Hedera* 'Marmorata' and I have also seen it listed as *Hedera canariensis* 'Marmorata'. Botanists have only recently raised the *azorica* to species rank.

Hedera hibernica

Until very recently, this has been a variety of *Hedera helix*, but botanists have postulated that this too, should be given a species rank. This is the large, green leaved ivy that one sees in hedgerows and on the forest floor, for it enjoys scrambling rather than climbing. It has two excellent variegated clones.

H. h. **'Maculata'** This is a vigorous, vining grower with triangular, 5-lobed leaves measuring anything up to 9cm by 14cm (3.5 by 5.5in). They are a good dark green with variously shaped markings of white and grey with dark green.

H. h. **'Variegata'** In this form, the same sized leaves can be entirely rich golden yellow or partly coloured, this colouring often being defined by a vein. Some leaves can be found with a degree of blotching of the yellow colouring.

In these last two variegated *hibernica* clones, it is essential to prune out the predominance of green leaves to maintain a plant with the colouring for which it was originally selected and named.

H. h. **'Sulphur Heart'** This ivy has an irregular shaped leaf, somewhat rumpled and distorted with a chartreuse to yellowish-green margin.

Fig 86 Hedera colchica *'Sulphur Heart'*
clothing a tree trunk.

Overall the leaves give the impression that they have been dusted with sulphur.

Ivies are the most versatile of climbers and are excellent for ground cover. Some of the more bushy and small leaved varieties are ideal for pots, urns and baskets and make very good plants to be grown in association with flowering shrubs and many herbaceous and perennial plants. Many forms of ivy will trail and hang down and are quite happy without any assistance for support. For those of you with chain link fencing, perhaps dividing your garden from your neighbour, ivies are excellent to produce a covered boundary.

A 'Fedge'

This is a coined word meaning a cross between a fence and a hedge and is the result obtained when ivies are planted at the foot of chain link fencing when they will climb, at first perhaps, needing a little tying in for encouragement. If mixed leaf patterns are included in the planting, there will very soon be an almost evergreen, impervious and attractive boundary. An annual clip over with a pair of shears or secateurs to encourage the covering capacity is all that is required.

An arbour can become more attractive when an ivy is planted at each side at the foot of the arbour, perhaps combined with a climbing rose or clematis. With both fedge and arbour, it may be necessary to cut back top growth which can bush out and become top heavy.

I have dwelt on the subject of ivy because I have a particular love for this plant. Ivies are so versatile, with the variety of leaf outlines and the almost evergreen colour, particularly with the variegated clones. Clones can be selected for leaves that are bright yellow, variegated and of a plum colour in winter.

I have been collecting and growing ivies for thirty years or more and have founded a society dedicated to the plant called The British Ivy Society. We work closely with The American Ivy Society and our aims and objectives are to disseminate information, to exchange plant material and also to form a register so that some of the most attractive and diverse forms of ivy will bear the same given name in all parts of the world.

ROSES

Roses suit many climates and can be grown in a variety of soils. They are readily available in most nurseries and can be chosen so that their flowers can be enjoyed over a long season, some also have the bonus of a heavy perfume. These are not expensive plants to buy and my research on roses has shown that it is the single most popular plant grown in this country and far outstrips the sales of any other plant genus.

In nature, rose species are confined almost exclusively to the Northern Hemisphere: Europe, North America and Northern Asia including China. Many of the several thousand different species known to botanists are not decorative enough for use in our gardens. However, several species have been cultivated and enjoyed for thousands of years. There are references to roses in ancient literature and *Rosa gallica* is alleged to have been grown by the Medes and Persians. Other species emanating from China have as long a history.

In western civilisations, the ancient Greeks and Romans both valued the rose, often using it as a symbol of beauty and as a token of love and to this day, there are record sales of red roses on St Valentine's Day. We also use, as did the Romans, rose petals to shower over guests at banquets and the bride and groom on their wedding day, though the use of confetti has much the same significance and origin.

In the late 1700s, the Empress Josephine became famous for the collection of roses displayed in her gardens. These gardens contained as many different kinds as she could gather together and such was her patronage that roses quickly became popular and this has not waned since. One must allow that she would not find many of the catalogues of today listing the roses of her time nor would she, if she were here today, recognise many of the diverse colours, growth habits and hybrid forms that we now enjoy.

The Latin phrase, *sub-rosa*, meaning under the rose, derives from the flower being the emblem of silence and was sculptured on the ceilings of banquet rooms to remind the guests that what was spoken there was not to be repeated.

Roses were the symbols during the Wars of the Roses, the red rose for the House of Lancaster and the white rose for the House of York. The colours were combined to form the badge for the House of Tudor. In recent times, the rose has become the national flower of the United States of America.

That great plantswoman, Gertrude Jekyll, in her book of 1902, *Roses for English Gardens* says, 'When they begin to grow freely among bushes and trees and if it is desired to lead the far searching growths one way or another, it is easily done with a long forked stick. It is like painting a picture with an immensely long handled brush for, with a 14ft pole with a forked end, one can guide the branches into a yew or holly or tall thorn into such forms of upright spring or downward swag as one pleases'. Often recommended for treatment in this manner is *Rosa filipes* 'Kiftsgate'. There is a gigantic specimen climbing to 15m (50ft) into a copper beech tree near Chipping Campden in Gloucestershire.

The growing of such roses into trees is very satisfying if space is available. However, in smaller gardens there are sturdy, newer roses in a variety of colours which will comfortably cover an arch or house wall. Climbing roses need to be grown with a dark background and there is no doubt that the effect of roses is much enhanced by large evergreens in the vicinity or dark green hedges.

Climbing Roses

The roses in this group are quite varied in their habit and vigour. Some flower only once a season while others flower successively or in flushes.

Regular pruning involves dead-heading, cutting back the leading shoots to control their vigour, and trimming back side shoots to 2–3 buds in the winter. With older plants, unproductive shoots can be completely cut out to make room for the new shoots developing from the base. Weak and

Fig 87   Rosa 'Cooperi'. An interesting rose suitable for a sheltered wall. This rose was raised from seed collected from the wild in Burma. The leaves are extremely glossy and the single flowers are of a unique pure white.

dead shoots should also be cut out. There is very little pruning required apart from cutting out very old, dead, weak or diseased wood.

Some of the more upright growing varieties look best trained to a post or pillar, twining the stems around it as they grow. Flowers will form near the tips of these shoots. Other roses flower more profusely if the stems can be trained horizontally, say to wires on a wall or fence. Blooms may then develop along the entire length of the stem, not just at the tips.

Roses are usually budded on to a wild rose rootstock. Shoots growing from this are called suckers. When these form, scrape away the soil and trace the sucker back to the root. Tear away the sucker and replace the soil.

Fig 88 Rosa 'Améthyste' (Syn. 'Rose-Marie Viaud'). A late flowering, rambling rose of great charm with small, double, amethyst coloured flowers.

The rose family are a most valuable group of plants with such a wide choice of colours, forms and habits, one can easily be found to suit most situations. Climbing roses have a vigorous habit and make ideal wall plants. Wires should be fastened to the wall on to which the stems can be trained. Ramblers look more at home in borders or island beds where they can be left to roam. However, they do take up a lot of space.

Sharp secateurs are an essential tool for rose pruning as a clean cut, correctly positioned and sloping slightly away from the bud is very important. Do remember that the cutting blade of secateurs will need sharpening and a sharpening stone is a worthwhile investment. Blunt secateurs will perform badly, tearing and crushing stems and causing die-back. Regular feeding as well as prompt attention to pests and disease control will reward you with the best of blooms.

Planting

Roses can be gross feeders and it is wise to follow the advice on preparation of the soil in Chapter 4. The recommended planting times for roses has always been November and December, though there are those who contend that this period can be extended to mid-April with equal success. If you are having your roses sent to you bare rooted during these months, it is as well to soak the roots thoroughly for an hour or two in a bucket of water before planting. If your roses are purchased from a garden centre in a container, again it is wise to ensure that the soil is thoroughly moist. Make sure that the hole made for the rose is sufficiently large to take all the roots when these are spread out.

With a container grown plant or a plant which has come bare rooted, one can usually see the soil level point on the stem. The planting depth should be 2cm (0.8in) below the point where the top growth meets the roots. It is wise to work in some fine soil between the roots, together with a little peat, trampling lightly on the soil with your feet around the stem. Do ensure that if you are planting in the late end of the recommended season, i.e. March or April, water thoroughly at intervals until the rose is established.

General Maintenance

You will probably not need to prune for the first two years. Subsequently, it is best to cut back the short side shoots that produced last year's flowers. Remove some of the older main growth and certainly any that are weak or dead. It is important to leave an elegant climber with sufficient but not too much growth to allow it to get too old and twiggy. Mulching once a year with manure or decayed compost is all that is needed, though if your soil is sandy and hungry, twice a year is recommended. A good organic based fertiliser or rose fertiliser as a dressing in March can also be recommended.

Most climbing roses will often survive happily without being affected by the two main diseases,

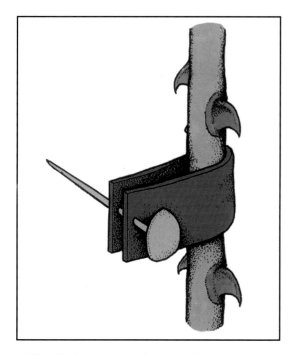

Fig 89   Climbing roses can be easily affixed to a wall or fence by using hardened steel nails and a leather or plastic strap.

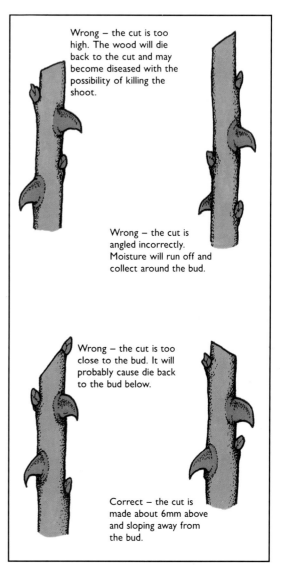

Wrong – the cut is too high. The wood will die back to the cut and may become diseased with the possibility of killing the shoot.

Wrong – the cut is angled incorrectly. Moisture will run off and collect around the bud.

Wrong – the cut is too close to the bud. It will probably cause die back to the bud below.

Correct – the cut is made about 6mm above and sloping away from the bud.

Fig 90   It is important to prune your climbing and rambling roses correctly. The accompanying sketch is intended to guide you. It is as well to train yourself to this procedure.

mildew and black spot. However, it is quite likely that you will probably have your fair share of greenfly and black fly – you should spray with a systemic insecticide as soon as these pests appear.

It is good husbandry to remove flower heads as soon as they die. If rose suckers appear, do try to cut them off as close to the base as possible. Try not to leave a stump but cut away a small heel from the root otherwise the sucker will appear again. Some rose growers say that it is possible to pull the sucker away, but to do this, one needs to remove the soil to see the point of attachment of the sucker to the root and then, with two hands gripping the sucker close to the point of union, give a sharp tug in order to tear the sucker from the root.

Pruning depends very much on the type of rose and the time of year to prune is the subject of much debate. Rambling roses, with the exception of the repeat flowering cultivars, should be pruned after flowering. Old and dead stems should be cut down to ground level. Climbing tea roses (sports) and large flowered climbers are best pruned in late winter. Such pruning should aim to control the growth of the rose and also to

Fig 91   Rosa moyesii 'Geranium'. A compact form, ideal for smaller gardens. The flowers are a brilliant red with larger hips than the type.

encompass the removal of old dead wood. It is good policy to cut long stems that are to be removed into short lengths as pruning proceeds, otherwise the dragging out of the old thorny stems could well damage young growth. Roses trained into trees are rarely pruned, mainly because of the difficulty in carrying out this task.

Introduction to the List of Selected Roses

No list of recommended roses can be complete. For some of the more unusual roses, use the specialist nurseries who, thankfully, are keeping alive many of the older named roses for the specialist, connoisseur and avid collector.

I have endeavoured to list those roses that are likely to be readily available from specialist growers and from the larger garden centres. It is advisable to order your roses in early summer so that, at lifting time which is usually late autumn, you do not find yourself on a waiting list for the rose of your choice.

Climbing roses use their thorns to attach themselves lightly to supports but in wind, they will be blown down unless they are carefully tied in. Think of them as scramblers, rather like brambles. They are in contrast to the free standing bushy roses commonly seen in gardens. There are scrambling roses which do not need tying in and these are usually grown into trees and the rose growth is held by the tree's branches and twigs. These usually give enough support to prevent the rose from falling, for example 'Kiftsgate'.

Very few roses will flower in permanent shade. However, their roots can be planted in the shade providing that their stems can grow into the sun. Roses like a sunny position and a very small number will tolerate semi-shade. Plant climbing roses at least 45cm (17in) away from a wall for, if too close, the roots can become very dry because the wall tends to keep the rain from the roots. If the rose is to be trained into a tree, it is best planted on the side towards the prevailing wind, so that the stems will be blown towards the tree. Air circulation on walls is important, especially for those varieties which are subject to mildew.

Roses will not tolerate waterlogged soils but if the soil is well balanced, they will grow equally well on sandy or clay soils. It is only when there is an excess of lime or acid in the soil that successful rose growing could be a problem to the gardener.

The roses listed here are a selection from the cultivars that are now available. As far as possible, they are grouped according to flower colour but this is not a rigid grouping. For instance, white may be a pure white, creamy white or a yellowy white.

Fig 92   Rosa 'Ballerina'. A hybrid musk rose with hydrangea-like heads of small, single, blossom pink flowers. Perpetual flowering well into the autumn.

Ramblers – Summer Flowering

Ramblers are not as popular now since the introduction of the repeat flowering climbing roses. These ramblers should not be expected to flower well until fully established.

'Albertine'   This has the appearance of a large, sprawly shrub. Foliage is shiny and the flowers are double and tawny pink which open from coppery red buds. Sweetly scented, flowers in mid summer.

'François Juranville'   A vigorous rambler with flat double flowers of coral pink, apple scented, and summer flowering.

'Paul Transon'   A lovely coral tea rose with small shiny leaves, richly tinted when young. Semi double flowers, apple scented and free flowering. Produces many late flowers.

'Paul's Himalayan Musk'   A vigorous rambler with small lilac pink fragrant flowers which are borne in clusters.

'Crimson Shower'   The double flowers open late and have a long flowering season. A good rambling rose but with little or no scent.

'Russelliana'   Flowers of deep cerise crimson, small, double and clustered. Very good colour effect at mid summer and has an old rose scent.

'Veilchenblau'   Flowers generously with buds of crimson purple. When open, has violet petals streaked with white. This is semi double and has a scent of green apples. Ideal for a shady wall and flowers early.

'Fécilité et Perpétue'   This is best grown over a low wall, tree stump or hedge. It is very bushy and at flowering time is covered with double flowers like rosettes, white from the buds which are touched with crimson. Has a delicate primrose scent.

'Sander's White Rambler'   A vigorous rambler and has a delightful scent. Small white flowers.

'Patricia Macoun'   This is an interesting hybrid rambler. It is covered in double cupped flowers of pure white in mid summer and is very fragrant.

'Wedding Day'   This is a prolific rambler and with a mass of flowers which have a strong orange fragrance. The buds are yellow and open to creamy white with orange-yellow stamens. An excellent variety for growing into trees.

Climbers – Repeat Flowering

In the earlier part of this century, an emergence of one or two varieties of climbing roses with remontant or repeat flowering characteristics has influenced much of the breeding of modern day climbers. As much of the plant's energy during the summer months is used in flower production, one must not expect quick luscious growth. Pruning therefore needs to be kept to a minimum and twiggy growth should be removed, keeping the plant trimmed to shape. These roses are ideal for screens, pergolas, pillars, walls and trellis.

'Swan Lake'   This rose has beautiful white flowers, flushed in the centre with a rosy colour. Glossy leaves but without fragrance in the blooms. May suffer from black spot.

'Golden Dawn, Climbing'   This rose has good foliage and the flowers are light yellow, double and with a lovely scent.

'Mermaid'   Vigorous growth with handsome glossy foliage. The large single flowers are pale sulphur yellow.

'Paul's Lemon Pillar'   This rose should be grown on a warm wall in cold districts. The flowers are very large and are a good lemon-white and very fragrant. Flowers in early mid summer.

'**Royal Gold**'   This should also be grown on sheltered walls. Blooms are a striking golden yellow, very large and scented. Can also be grown as a loose shrub.

'**Compassion**'   This rose has very good dark glossy foliage and is a vigorous grower. The lovely buds are a warm apricot and open to a soft salmon-pink. Very fragrant and has continuous flowers.

'**Mrs Sam McGredy, Climbing**'   The foliage on this rose is mahogany tinted. The flowers are fragrant and are a splendid deep salmon-pink shaded with coppery-red.

'**Zéphirine Drouhin**'   This is the thornless rose. The medium size blooms are carmine-pink and have a sweet fragrance. It is prone to mildew but it can be fairly easily controlled with regular spraying.

'**Ena Harkness, Climbing**'   The nodding crimson blooms on this rose are fragrant and large.

'**Crimson Glory, Climbing**'   This splendid rose has deep crimson flowers and is very fragrant. It should be placed out of the hottest sun as the colour is rather purplish and can look too harsh in strong light.

'**Chaplin's Pink Climber**'   This has vigorous, somewhat rambling growth. The flowers are a strong pink and are semi double.

'**Cécile Brunner, Climbing**'   This is a vigorous climber bearing masses of tiny clear pink flowers which are fragrant.

'**Danse Du Feu**'   This vigorous climber will grow on a north wall. It has semi-double blooms of bright orange-red.

'**Flaming Sunset, Climbing**'   The very fragrant flowers on this rose are a deep orange and the foliage is a glossy bronze.

Fig 93   Rosa '*Parkdirektor Riggers*'. A Kordesii hybrid rose which has strong stems and is repeat flowering. The flowers are of a velvety crimson and are borne in large clusters.

'**Joseph's Coat**'   This rose has yellow-orange and red semi-double flowers. Can also be grown as a shrub.

'**Independence, Climbing**'   The double shapely flowers are vivid vermillion, softened by subtle coppery and metallic tints. Slightly fragrant, flowers fully double.

ANNUAL CLIMBERS

These are plants often neglected in the average garden but they provide a wealth of colour and interest and are best treated as half hardy annuals.

The seed should be obtained from nurserymen or from garden shops and the instructions on the packets observed. However, as a general rule, seeds should be started in pots indoors or preferably in a greenhouse. This will enable young plants to be planted out in open ground after the last week in May in the south, or two weeks later, in June, in the north.

The sites chosen for planting should be against sunny walls or in large tubs standing against such walls. A few short twigs, pea sticks or similar material, placed around the plants to give them support, can be advantageous at planting time.

Annual climbing plants can be grown with great success when associated with more permanent plants. The annuals will climb up and through such plants and will become attached to the upper branches by the time that the flowering stage has been reached. Where perennial climbers have been planted against a wall, there may be some gaps that are not completely clothed. Annual climbers can be used to fill these spaces and the extra shelter and protection will provide good growing conditions for some of the half hardy annuals.

ACONITUM Ranunculaceae (Monkshood)

If you haven't already got one of these plants, they are easy to raise from seed.

A. volubile This plant has been dealt with more fully in the main list as it is more usually treated as a perennial.

COBAEA Cobaeaceae (Cup and Saucer Creeper)

C. scandens Mexico. There are very nearly twenty species hailing from Central and South

Fig 94   The flower of Cobaea scandens.

America. Seed is sown *in situ* or started earlier in the year in pots in a greenhouse. It will grow and climb by tendrils to 4m (13ft) or more in one season. It provides most attractive flowers that resemble a cup and saucer. Their colour is greenish-white with the rim and throat of the cup deepening to violet. The flowers appear from July to October.

There is a *Cobaea scandens* 'Alba' and a variegated form that used to be more readily available from seedsmen some years ago. Its pinnate leaves, composed of 4–6 ovate to elliptical leaflets each 10cm (4in) long, are edged with a wide band of white. This is an ideal climber for a pergola or over an archway whose site is not too windy or it can be trained up trellis or wires.

CUCURBITA *Cucurbitaceae* (Ornamental Gourds)

If you have the space, gourds are excellent half hardy climbers with fruits of various shapes, sizes and colours. Almost invariably they are listed under their species name or in seed catalogues as 'Mixed Gourds'. Give the plants all the sun that you can and tie them in as they grow. Do not allow the fruit to lie on the ground as they are loved by slugs. Harvest the gourds on a warm, dry day in early October and lay in a warm room to completely ripen. They can then be painted with a clear varnish and used for decoration in the house.

ECCREMOCARPUS *Bignoniaceae* (Chilean Glory Flower)

E. scaber   This plant has been dealt with in the main list for it truly is a perennial. Sow the seed in boxes or pots placed on a window sill or in the greenhouse if you have one. Plant out after frosts.

HUMULUS *Cannabidaceae* (Hop)

Although this is a perennial, in this country it is more usual to treat it as a half hardy annual. Raise from seed obtained from seedsmen.

H. japonicus 'Variegatus'   This plant makes considerable growth in a season and is ideal for trellis, walls, fences, arbours and pergolas.

IPOMOEA *Convolvulaceae* (Morning Glory)

Under this heading, many similar climbers are grouped.

I. purpurea   Seedsmen sell packets of mixed colour flower forms such as 'Flying Saucers', 'Wedding Bells' and 'Pearly Gates'. This plant will make a dense screening climber for covering trellis and chain link fences. It bears a profusion of gorgeous trumpet-shaped flowers, some as big as 10cm (4in) long and as much in diameter.

Fig 95   The flower of Ipomoea.

Fig 96 Tropaeolum *'Alaska'. The variegated annual nasturtium.*

Fig 97 Tropaeolum *'Alaska'.*

Flowers freely the first year from seed. Sow the seed in peat pots to avoid root disturbance and when planting out, place the whole pot and plant straight into the ground. The roots will penetrate the peat pot and the peat will eventually be absorbed.

LATHYRUS Leguminosae
(Annual sweet pea)

It is more usual to see these plants grown and trained up bamboo canes arranged in long rows or grown up canes tied together at the top to form a wigwam. As an alternative, it can be fun to grow them at the foot of a more permanent wall shrub or climber or wherever you have enough space with good, rich soil and plenty of sun. A few short twigs or pea sticks or similar material, placed around the plants, will give them support at planting time. They will add a spot of colour to an area where, perhaps, the spring flowers are already over.

The seeds of sweet peas should be started in the autumn, overwintering them in a frame or buy in the plants from a nursery in the spring. To prolong the flowering period, do remove the dead or dying flowers which will prevent the plant from using up its energy by producing seed pods.

PUERARIA Leguminosae
(Kudzu Vine)

This is a native of China and Japan and has good covering power for a wall or shed. It climbs to about 4m (13ft) in a season and has light purple pea-like flowers. The foliage is trifoliate. This climber should be raised from seed and planted out when frost is past. It will produce a rapid cover.

RHODOCHITON Scrophulariacea

R. atrosanguineum   This is a tender climber and supports itself by twisting flower and leaf stalks. It will grow up to a height of 2m (6.5ft).

The tubular flowers are dark blood red and are 5cm (2in) long with five prominent lobes. The solitary flowers have a calyx which is broadly bell-shaped and is of a different red which adds to the beauty of the flowers. These bloom in the first season when grown from seed.

THUNBERGIA Acanthaceae
(Black-eyed Susan)

This is not a tall climber, only rising to 1m (3.3ft) or so. However, it is an excellent half hardy stem twiner. It has the well-known name of 'Black-eyed Susan' for the flowers are tubular, widely expanding to a bell-like mouth. There are several colour varieties though the usual one is yellow. It takes its name from the dark purple throat of the flower.

TROPAEOLUM Tropaeolaceae
(Canary Creeper)

T. peregrinum   This is the ever-popular Canary Creeper, the leaves of which are deeply cut into lobes and the yellow flowers resemble a bird in flight. The plants should be raised from seed and planted out in poor soil when frosts are past.

T. majus   The climbing nasturtium with many varieties of flower colour. Sow the seed in late spring where you intend to grow it or start in pots. Tropaeolums prefer a poor soil and if planted in rich soil will grow too much leaf and produce few flowers.

T. 'Golden Gleam'   This is a semi-climber and when grown in a pot, makes a fine, decorative plant if it is trained on bamboo canes made into the shape of a wigwam by tying several canes together at the top.

T. 'Alaska'   A bushy nasturtium whose foliage is evenly marbled with white. The flower colours range from orange, yellow and apricot. It makes a good eye-catching sight when in flower and planted around the edges of a pot or tub.

CHAPTER 7

Plants for Particular Sites

The lists of plants are for general guidance and the plant descriptions in the main lists will help you to make your choice, for a special place, for colour, perfume or foliage interest.

Fig 98   Jasminum stephanensis

North and East Walls

Akebia
Azara
Berberidopsis
Chaenomeles
Clematis alpina
Clematis macropetala
Clematis montana
Cotoneaster horizontalis
Hedera
Hydrangea
Jasminum officinale
Lathyrus
Lonicera tragophylla
Parthenocissus
Rosa (see list)
Tropaeolum speciosum

Many of the above plants will undoubtedly grow quite satisfactorily on south facing walls.

South Walls

The plants listed below are those that prefer or need south facing walls in the colder parts of the country.

Abelia
Abeliophyllum
Abutilon
Actinidia kolomikta
Campsis
Carpenteria

Fig 99 Carpentaria californica

Fig 100 Hedera helix *'Goldheart'* best clipped back.

Cestrum
Chaenomeles
Chimonanthus
Choisya
Clematis (see list)
Crinodendron
Cytisus battandierii
Decumaria
Desfontainea
Eccremocarpus
Fatsia
Ficus
Fremontodendron
Hoheria
Ipomoea

Jasminum
Kadsura
Lapageria
Mutisia
Passiflora
Perovskia
Phlomis
Phygelius
Punica
Robinia
Rosa (see list)
Rubus
Senecio
Solanum
Trachelospermum

119

Fig 101 Eucryphia x 'Nymansay'. *A vigorous evergreen, a chance hybrid between* E. cordifolia *and* E. glutinosa *from the gardens of Nymans in Sussex, flowering in August. This plant will tolerate a chalky soil.*

Wattakaka
Wisteria

Evergreen and Semi-Evergreen Plants

Berberidopsis
Cestrum
Choisya ternata
Clianthus
Coronilla
Cotoneaster
Crinodendron
Decumaria
Eleagnus
Eucryphia
Euonymus
Ficus

Fremontodendron (partially evergreen)
Garrya elliptica
Hedera
Hoheria sexstylosa
Holboellia
Hypericum leschenaultii
Itea ilicifolia
Kadsura
Lapageria
Osmanthus
Phlomis
Pileostegia
Plumbago
Pyracantha
Smilax aspera
Solanum crispum (semi-evergreen)
Trachelospermum
Veronica hulkeana (partially evergreen)

Variegated Plants

Abelia × *grandiflora* 'Frances Mason'
Abelia × *grandiflora* 'Gold Strike'
Abutilon megapotamicum 'Variegatum'
Abutilon × *milleri*
Abutilon striatum
Acanthopanax sieboldiana 'Variegatus'
Actinidia kolomikta
Actinidia polygama
Ampelopsis brevipedunculata 'Elegans'
Azara macrophylla 'Variegata'
Berchemia racemosa 'Variegata'
Campsis radicans 'Flava'
Choisya ternata 'Sundance'
Cobaea scandens 'Variegata'
Coronilla glauca 'Variegata'
Cotoneaster horizontalis 'Variegata'
Euonymus fortuneii – variegated forms

Fig 102   A good use of pots to soften the sharp angle of a wall.

Fig 103   A good example of architectural planting, the close clipped shrub contrasting with the trails of the vine on the corner of the house wall.

Fatsia japonica – variegated form
Feijoa sellowiana 'Variegata'
Ficus pumila 'Variegata'
Fuchsia – variegated forms
Hedera colchica 'Dentata Variegata'
Hedera rhombea 'Variegata'
Hoheria – variegated form
Humulus lupulus 'Aureus'
Humulus japonicus 'Variegatus'
Jasminum – various variegated forms
Kadsura japonica 'Variegata'
Lonicera japonica 'Aureoreticulata'
Myrtus communis 'Variegata'
Myrtus communis tarentina 'Variegata'
Osmanthus – variegated forms
Philadelphus coronarius 'Aureus'
Philadelphus coronarius 'Variegatus'

Fig 104   A well-clothed wall and trellis with various climbing plants.

Fig 105   Clematis florida 'Sieboldii' (florida bicolour).

Fig 106 Lonicera serotina.

Philadelphus 'Innocence'
Rhamnus alaternus 'Variegata'
Rubus fruticosus 'Variegatus'
Smilax aspera var. *maculata*
Solanum capsicastrum 'Variegatum'
Solanum dulcamara 'Variegatum'
Trachelospermum jasminoides 'Variegatum'
Trachelospermum jasminoides 'Tricolor'
Tropaeolum nanum 'Alaska'
Wattakaka sinensis 'Variegata'

Plants with Scented Flowers

Everyone has a different appreciation of fragrance and weather conditions can affect the degree and intensity of the perfume, therefore comparisons between cultivars are rather difficult to make. It is probable that dressings of potash will encourage flower production and help the wood to ripen and will also enrich the perfume of the flowers.

Fig 107   Rosa moyesii 'Geranium'

Fig 108   Rosa 'Mermaid'. The large single
flowers have wide, elegant petals with amber
coloured stamens. It repeat flowers constantly
throughout the summer.

Abeliophyllum
Actinidia kolomikta
Akebia
Azara macrophylla
Choisya ternata
Coronilla glauca
Cytisus battandieri
Holboellia latifolia
Jasminum

Lathyrus odoratus
Lonicera
Myrtus
Osmanthus
Philadelphus
Rosa (many varieties – see list)
Trachelospermum
Wisteria

Glossary

Adventitious   Roots arising from other parts of the plant than the seed. Usually implies roots on aerial stems.

Aerial Root   A root originating above ground level.

Anther   Pollen-bearing part of the stamen.

Aphis   The scientific name for aphids, a common insect pest of roses. Their food is obtained by sucking the juices of the plant.

Axil   Angle formed by a leaf or lateral branch with the stem.

Bicolour   Having two distinct colours.

Bipinnate   When the leaf is pinnate, the divisions are also pinnate.

Bract   Modified leaf at the base of a flower stalk or flower cluster.

Calyx   Collective term for the flower sepals.

Corolla   Collective term for the flower petals.

Corymb   Flat-topped or rounded flowerhead with outer petals opening first.

Cultivar   Garden variety of a plant of a form found in the wild and maintained in cultivation.

Cyme   Flat-topped or rounded flowerhead with the outer flowers the first to open.

Deciduous   With leaves that seasonally fall.

Double   Flowers with more than the usual number of petals.

Evergreen   Remaining green throughout the winter.

Family   Group of genera with important characteristics in common, e.g. *Rosaceae*, the rose family.

Fungicide   A chemical used to kill fungi that, e.g. on roses, cause diseases such as mildew, black spot or rust.

Heeling in   Temporary planting before permanent placing.

Humus   Organic matter that is well rotted.

Hybrid   A cross between different species, sub species or varieties.

Insecticide   Any substance that will kill insects and, by extension, mites and other pests.

Mulch   A dressing of organic matter applied to the surface of the soil to assist its water retention and suppress the growth of annual weeds.

Node   The point on a stem where the leaves arise.

Panicle   A stalked flower cluster branching from a central stem.

Petiole   The stalk by which the leaf is attached to the stem.

Fig 109   Colourful foreground planting to walls well clothed with climbers and framing a doorway.

Pinnate   With leaves arranged on each side of the same stalk.

Raceme   Simple elongated inflorescence with stalked flowers.

Scandent   With climbing stems.

Semi-evergreen   Losing some or all leaves in severe weather.

Spent hops   A good source of organic material. The residue left from brewing.

Sport   A mutation arising from genetic changes in a plant or part of a plant. It can cause variation in growth habit or change of leaf colour or flower colour.

Spur   A short branch or shoot.

Stamen   The pollen-bearing organ of a flower.

Stipules   Leaf-like appendages at the base of a flower stalk, usually in pairs.

Tendril   The twining, leafless part of the plant which attaches itself to any structure so as to support the plant.

Tuber   A fleshy thickening or outgrowth of an underground stem from which new plants arise. It acts as a storage system.

Index